MARILYN MONROE

MARILYN MONROE
THE LAST INTERVIEW
and OTHER CONVERSATIONS

with an introduction by SADY DOYLE

MELVILLEHOUSE
BROOKLYN • LONDON

MARILYN MONROE: THE LAST INTERVIEW
AND OTHER CONVERSATIONS

Copyright © 2020 by Melville House Publishing

Introduction © 2020 by Sady Doyle

"The 1951 Model Blonde" by Robert Cahn. First published in
Collier's Magazine, September 8, 1951. Reprinted with permission of
Collier's Magazine, a registered trademark of JTE Multimedia,
435 Devon Park Drive, Wayne, PA, 19087.

"Quizzing Marilyn Monroe" by Helen Hover. First published
in *Motion Picture Magazine*, January 1954. Reprinted with permission
of the Estate of Helen Hover Weller.

"The New Marilyn Monroe" by Pete Martin. First published in
The Saturday Evening Post, May 5, 1956. Reprinted with permission of
the Estate of William Thornton "Pete" Martin Jr.

Conversations with Marilyn by William J. Weatherby. First published by
Paragon House, 1992. Reprinted with permission of Paragon House.

"A Last Long Talk with a Lonely Girl" by Richard Meryman © 1962
The Picture Collection, Inc. All rights reserved. Reprinted/Translated
from *Life* and published with permission of The Picture Collection, Inc.

Reproduction in any manner in any language in whole or
in part without written permission is prohibited.

First Melville House printing: June 2020

Melville House Publishing   8 Blackstock Mews
46 John Street   and   Islington
Brooklyn, NY 11201   London N4 2BT

mhpbooks.com   facebook.com/mhpbooks   @melvillehouse

ISBN: 978-1-61219-877-4
ISBN: 978-1-61219-878-1 (eBook)

Printed in the United States of America

1   3   5   7   9   10   8   6   4   2

A catalog record for this book is available from the Library of Congress.

CONTENTS

xi   INTRODUCTION BY SADY DOYLE

3   THE 1951 MODEL BLONDE
     Conversation with Robert Cahn
     Collier's Magazine
     September 8, 1951

23   QUIZZING MARILYN MONROE
     Interview with Helen Hover
     Motion Picture Magazine
     January 1954

33   THE NEW MARILYN MONROE
     Conversation with Pete Martin
     The Saturday Evening Post
     May 5, 1956

61   CONVERSATIONS WITH MARILYN
     Conversation with William J. Weatherby
     Conversations with Marilyn
     1961 [first published in 1976]

91   THE LAST INTERVIEW: "A LAST LONG
     TALK WITH A LONELY GIRL"
     Conversation with Richard Meryman
     Life
     August 17, 1962

INTRODUCTION

SADY DOYLE

"I always see that in interviews," Marilyn Monroe once said, mid-interview. "The questions demand certain answers and make you seem a certain kind of person. The questions often tell more about the interviewer than the answers do about me."

It is not new to say that Marilyn Monroe spent her life, and her afterlife, as a projection of other people's fantasies. "We told [everybody] what the deal was," one of the Hollywood publicity agents who launched her told the *Saturday Evening Post* in 1956. "We said, 'We think this girl has a great future; she's beautiful, her chassis is great, and are you interested?' Each guy had his own idea of what he wanted, and he let his imagination play upon her. This is the way such things get done."

The men in question imagined Marilyn into being the midcentury's most famous sex symbol; a deeply serious actress who was pilloried for taking acting classes; and a spectacularly funny comedian who never got credit for being in on the joke, even as she wrote all her own best lines. (Several are included here. On the fake studio backstory that she had been discovered while working as a babysitter, she said that "you'd think that they would have used a little more imagination and have had me at least a daddy sitter"; of her early pinup photos, which had her posing by the ocean, she noted that "you looked at those pictures and you didn't see much ocean, but you saw a lot of me.") Monroe was so effortlessly quotable that, decades after her death, the "Fake Viral Marilyn Monroe Quote" has become a social plague. Anything at the intersection of "empowering" and girly—"if you can't handle me at my worst, you don't deserve me at my best"; "give a girl the right shoes and she can conquer the world"; "it's better to be absolutely ridiculous than absolutely boring"; and so on—winds up attributed to her and slapped up on Instagram after being photoshopped over a smiling picture of her face.

Marilyn Monroe was a sharp observer of her own persona, and surely she would see the irony: the "empowering," quasi-feminist Marilyn Monroe of so many Pinterest boards is just another projected fantasy, no more accurate than the dumb blonde or the obliging sexpot. She's famous for things she never said, after a lifetime of being denied the right to speak for herself.

*

The extent to which Marilyn Monroe was defined by the gaze of others is apparent throughout this book. Monroe—whose fame predates our current mania for the celebrity Q and A format, though she was no stranger to the paparazzi pile-on with its bulbs flashing and microphones being thrust in her face—is presented to us mostly through long profiles. The reporter is always given the chance to editorialize and tell us what he thinks of her; he's always a main character in the story, even if the character he's portraying always seems to be "guy who flirted with Marilyn Monroe."

The basics of Monroe's persona were evident from the beginning. We first meet her in a 1951 *Collier's* profile by Robert Cahn, which gives her exact weight and measurements before bothering to quote her, and calls her "the standard Hollywood Blonde, traditionally equipped with automatic batting eyelashes, a vague smile that seems to include everybody, and a head filled with sawdust."

Yet even then, there was discomfort in the characterization—a sense that, as one friend told Cahn, "Marilyn's soul just doesn't fit her body." Sure, there was tragedy; Monroe, born Norma Jean Mortenson, was the daughter of a mentally ill single mother, and was effectively orphaned when her mother was declared an unfit parent. She was passed among many foster homes; neglected, abandoned, and sexually abused by not one, but several of the men who had her in their care. The men who looked at the adult Marilyn often found her damage titillating: "Her natural beauty plus her inferiority complex gave her a look of mystery," says the man who shot her screen test. The one thing better than a beautiful girl was a beautiful, sad girl who might greet you as a savior.

Far more threatening was the fact that Marilyn Monroe was *smart*. Even when barely cared for and tossed around between abusive homes, Norma Jean won writing prizes at school. She performed so well academically that she was allowed to skip seventh grade. One of the key scandals of her very scandalous career—and if you doubt me, consider that it comes up multiple times, just in this book alone—was the fact that she said she wanted to star as Grushenka in *The Brothers Karamazov*, and thereby admitted that she had read *The Brothers Karamazov*, and thereby, perhaps even more damningly, admitted that she could read.

Monroe knew the performance expected of her—"any girl who resents [being whistled at] should live on a desert island," she said, disempoweringly, to *Motion Picture Magazine* in 1954—but her intelligence kept bumping up against the limits of her role until she left Los Angeles to take classes at The Actors Studio in New York. She began showing up in public wearing glasses, tucking her hair back in a ponytail, and reading books. All of the industry's contempt for her came gushing out at once.

It is brutal to read the things Monroe's male colleagues said about her. "She's sincerely trying to improve herself," *Some Like It Hot* and *The Seven Year Itch* director Billy Wilder told the *Saturday Evening Post*, before moving in for the kill: "If she sets out to be artistic and dedicated, and she carries it so far that she's willing to wear Sloppy-Joe sweaters and go without makeup and let her hair hang straight as a string, this is not what has made her great to date." Later in the same profile, the author consults the Hollywood PR man about the trauma he's incurred by witnessing Marilyn Monroe with—gasp—*no makeup.* His answer expands to include all of womankind, or at least all actresses: "If their hair isn't touched up and coiffured exactly right; if they're not gowned perfectly and their makeup is not one hundred percent, they look gruesome . . . They're created blondes, and when you create a blonde you have to complete your creation with makeup and dramatic clothes, otherwise you've got only part of an assembly job."

Monroe was achingly aware of herself as a created blonde, maybe *the* Created Blonde: a creature pieced together out of makeup and gowns and breathy giggles and clever jokes disguised as "dumb" slipups. She was an actress, and a great one, and her reward for creating one of the most indelible characters of the twentieth century was to be dismissed as a mere "personality." The question Marilyn Monroe had, as her brief life rushed toward its conclusion, was whether the woman who had created the blonde would ever get to play anybody else. It was an end foretold in the beginning: "Hollywood blondes," says that 1951 *Collier's* profile, "are generally considered the industry's most expendable item."

*

Marilyn Monroe died by suicide at the age of thirty-six. It is only now, as I begin to outlive her, that I realize how crushingly young that was. The tragedy has been so exhaustively bewailed and romanticized and fetishized—*it seems to me you lived your life,* yadda yadda—that it has come to seem another fantasy projection: a girl too good and gentle for this world simply folding in on herself and giving up once no one wanted her any more. Monroe herself wondered about the gender politics of her fragility: "I don't think it would be very feminine to be tough," she said, in her final interview with Richard Meryman, titled "A Last Long Talk with a Lonely Girl" when it ran in article form in *Life* two weeks after she died. "Guess I'll settle for the way I am."

Yet there was a toughness in Norma Jean, as she entered her midthirties. There was a defiance—an outright rage, in fact—that she was increasingly unable to keep under wraps. Her politics were beginning to peek out; asked if her blondeness made her a symbol of the beauty of the white race, she angrily rejected the idea that she ought to be "busty Miss Anne." Her queerness, long rumored, became something she would casually admit to in the middle of an interview: "No sex is wrong if there's love in it." She had begun her career telling women who objected to harassment that they should move to a desert island. She ended it feeling weary of being objectified and questioning her own investment in patriarchal ideas of fulfillment: "For years I thought having a father and being married meant happiness," she said to William Weatherby. "I've never had a father—you can't *buy* them!— but I've been married three times and haven't found permanent happiness yet."

"My body turned all these people on, like turning on an electric light, and there was so rarely anything human in it," she told Weatherby. "Marilyn Monroe became a burden, a— what do you call it?—an albatross. People expected so much of me, I sometimes hated them."

I hated them. That's not the voice of a drowned kitten or a passive Ophelia. That is the voice of a woman who is

rightfully, righteously pissed. What would change if we en-
visioned a Marilyn Monroe who was not tragic, but *angry*:
a queer Marilyn, an anti-racist Marilyn, a feminist Marilyn
who has learned exactly what is expected of the ideal woman
and is fucking sick of it?

Or am I just one more person projecting my desires onto
Marilyn Monroe? Her death blurs out the conclusion of her
story, keeps me from knowing what kind of woman she would
have become. Marilyn Monroe is frozen in time, which makes
her immortal—goddesses never have fortieth birthdays—but
robs her of the human complexity she longed for.

"When I was a kid, the world often seemed a pretty grim
place. I loved to escape through games and make-believe,"
Marilyn Monroe said. "You can do that even better as an
actress, but sometimes it seems you escape altogether and
people never let you come back. You're trapped in your fame.
Maybe I'll never get out of it now until it's over."

Marilyn Monroe has been dead for over half a century,
and it is not over yet. We are still right where we started: everyone loves her, no one knows her, and now, no one ever will.
We have only these interviews: only the girl peeking out behind the dumb blonde and the sexpot and the scandal, daring
us to set aside our own desires long enough to hear her out.

MARILYN MONROE

THE 1951 MODEL BLONDE

BLONDE

CONVERSATION WITH ROBERT CAHN
COLLIER'S MAGAZINE
SEPTEMBER 8, 1951

She's filmdom's Marilyn Monroe: Miss Cheesecake to GIs, whistle-bait in the studios—and an actress on her way up.

It was the kind of family party that Hollywood studios periodically throw for their outlying salesmen and picture-exchange executives in order to whoop up enthusiasm for the company's forthcoming product. The Cafe de Paris, more simply known as the 20th Century-Fox commissary, was crowded with a cheery assemblage of studio bigwigs and freshly manicured salesmen. For five days, in an atmosphere of backslapping camaraderie, the guests had watched the celluloid unroll, the same films which they were expected to describe as colossal and mean it. Now as a final lift to their morale the visitors were meeting, over highballs and hors d'oeuvres, such marquee names as Susan Hayward, Jeanne Crain, June Haver, Anne Baxter, Gregory Peck and Tyrone Power.

The party had fallen into small groups, one star per group, and at the bar a weary press agent was asking for his fifth highball when he glanced toward the doorway where

Marilyn Monroe, a recently acquired studio starlet, had just arrived. Amid a slowly gathering hush, she stood there, a blonde apparition in a strapless black cocktail gown, a little breathless as if she were Cinderella just stepped from a pumpkin coach. At that moment, the salesmen's esprit de corps took a sudden leap upward.

The press agent put down his drink. "I'd better get over and get the introductions started," he remarked to a colleague. "Stand by for the massacre."

He was too late. Already a studio vice-president and two producers, suddenly self-designated Prince Charmings, had converged on the late arrival. A moment later she was wafted off by the upper echelons, her progress punctuated by the popping of flash bulbs as the visitors pressed forward to have their pictures taken with her. Finally, as the guests sat down for dinner, the blonde was installed at the head of the No. 1 table, at the right hand of company president Spyros Skouras.

While the long-established female stars silently measured her, young Marilyn Monroe, who has logged less than fifty minutes' screen time, stole the show.

Sitting there, her chin resting prettily on the backs of her fingers, Marilyn looked the part of the standard Hollywood Blonde, traditionally equipped with automatic batting eyelashes, a vague smile that seems to include everybody, and a head filled with sawdust. Certainly her 118 pounds, handsomely distributed throughout her five-foot five-inch frame, are from the classic mold—bust, 37 inches; waist, 23 inches; hips, 34 inches. So sumptuous are Miss Monroe's dimensions that long before most people knew her name, her anonymous body was used to exploit the pictures in which she briefly appeared.

But all that is misleading. Marilyn is a beautiful blonde, but she is not a vacuous one. Her film experience is sharply limited, but her potential as a sensitive actress is not. Unlike many of her assembly-line predecessors, Marilyn has given clear indications that the 1951 model Hollywood blonde is custom-built.

This has been apparent in her movie appearances, brief as they have been. Only once in a producer's blue moon does there appear a blonde who brings to the screen a special in-delible vitality, and not simply the empty prettiness that the audience forgets as it leaves the theater. Marilyn Monroe is not a girl anyone quickly forgets. While Hollywood blondes are generally considered the industry's most expendable item, Miss Monroe's value during the past year has risen faster than the cost of living.

BIT ROLE ATTRACTS NOTICE

After looking on Marilyn merely as whistle-bait for four years, the film capital became abruptly aware of her last year at the first screening of John Huston's *The Asphalt Jungle*. Audi-ences of professional people perked up noticeably when the camera switched to a sofa filled by a recumbent blonde in tight-fitting, one-piece lounging pajamas. When the reclin-ing form stirred enough to walk, talk and even kiss "Uncle

Lon," played by Louis Calhern, there were murmurings in the projection room, as the watchers tried to discover the identity of the newcomer; she had not been listed at the beginning of the picture. This same lack was to trouble many another audience. Soon after the picture's release, Marilyn received a fan letter from a Midwest college fraternity.

"A bunch of us fellows went down to see *Asphalt Jungle*," they wrote. "And when you came on the screen we almost lost our eyeballs. We didn't even know who you were."

People have rapidly been finding out. Even in *All About Eve*, surrounded by one of the best casts Hollywood has assembled in recent years, Marilyn won more than her share of attention in the small role of the dumb blonde introduced by George Sanders as "a graduate of the Copacabana School of Dramatic Arts." More recently, with ears cocked to the whistles and wolf calls that have greeted Miss Monroe's appearance as the provocative secretary in *As Young As You Feel*, shrewd exhibitors have begun for the first time to put her name on their theater marquees.

Hollywood's hearing is no less acute. Today, spurred by Marilyn's impact on audiences, Fox press agents are in the midst of the biggest publicity build-up since the Jane Russell campaign. During the past twelve months, the studio's press department has sent out more than three thousand pictures of Marilyn to newspapers alone. In Germany the editors of *Stars and Stripes* have selected her "Miss Cheesecake of 1951," and in Korea her pinups swiftly were rated as the choicest wallpaper obtainable.

Like a famous predecessor, Jean Harlow, Marilyn's name is rapidly becoming the current Hollywood definition of sex appeal. After reading a Soviet attack on poems which have romantic ardor without social significance, one Hollywood columnist, Jim Henaghan, boldly suggested, "Let's drop a handful of pictures of Marilyn Monroe on them and see what happens."

Even on a sound stage among actors, to whom there is little new under the sun, Marilyn is a disturbing influence. During the filming of *Love Nest*, scheduled for release in a few weeks, Marilyn caused a small crisis when she appeared in a red and white polka-dot Bikini bathing suit described by one observer as having "hardly enough room for the polka dots." Miraculously gathered by the grapevine, so many studio employees crowded the set that director Joe Newman, without enough space to move his actors, was forced to bar all visitors.

The following day another scene required Marilyn to enter her apartment and leisurely disrobe for a shower unaware that the hero, Bill Lundigan, was asleep on a couch in the room.

Just as Marilyn had stripped to her flimsy underthings, director Newman bellowed: "Cut!"

Marilyn looked startled. "Did I do something wrong?" she asked innocently.

"No, honey," replied Newman. "You were perfect. But Lundigan was peeking."

Warmed by these spontaneous demonstrations of Miss Monroe's appeal, Fox executives are eagerly searching for new and combustible roles for her. Proceeding cautiously by placing Miss Monroe in smaller roles to gain experience, the studio chiefs are keeping their fingers crossed. They hope they have another Harlow. Even production chief Darryl Zanuck has gone on record: "Miss Monroe is the most exciting new personality in Hollywood in a long time."

Officials at Fox are quick to change the subject, however, when it is mentioned that the studio discovered Miss Monroe five years ago, dropped her contract after one eventful year, and then scrambled to return her to the fold after a rival studio had proved in *The Asphalt Jungle* that she could do more than adorn backgrounds and pose for cheesecake.

Wrong guesses about Marilyn are nothing new. Her greatest handicap, odd as it seems, is her face and figure, which automatically have typed her as the brainless sort. A few persons who have looked a little closer have seen, behind the panchromatic makeup and the studied, protective starlet mannerisms, a face on which twenty-three years of living have written several anguished chapters. Sometimes, behind the false eyelashes, comes the look of a lost child.

For most of her life, Marilyn was a lost child, with no family of her own—just a long succession of strange households that offered her food and shelter of various sorts, and little else. During the greater part of her childhood she was a public ward; her name then was Norma Jean Baker. She was a thin, sad-faced little girl of five, living with foster parents in an industrial suburb of Los Angeles, when she was first told that her father had been killed in an automobile accident before she was born, and that her mother had become too ill to take care of her.

This first household was a religious, austere one; dancing, smoking, movies and playing cards were considered "works of the devil." Yet a few months later, transferred to the equally modest home of a pair of Hollywood extras, she was taught to play cards and taken to picture shows. Eager to discover her talents, the movie-struck "parents" asked if she could dance. Norma Jean obligingly wiggled through her versions of a Spanish fandango, a hula-hula, and a sailor's hornpipe, all of which looked alike. She was desperately hurt when her new guardians laughed aloud.

Although little Norma Jean tried often and hard to please her assorted parents, she was to meet with many another rebuff. During her nomadic childhood she was to confront the restrictions, prejudices and peculiarities of twelve different families before she was sixteen.

There was the Christmas when Norma Jean was given a part in the class play, only to lose it when her current foster mother, fearing she would forget her lines and embarrass the family, asked the teacher to give it to someone else. Or the Easter when she was on a stage for the first time, as one of fifty black-robed youngsters forming a cross at [the] Hollywood Bowl.

"We all had on white tunics under the black robes," Marilyn recalls, "and at a given signal we were supposed to throw off the robes, changing the cross from black to white. But I got so interested in the people, the orchestra and the hills that I forgot to watch the conductor for the signal. And there I was—the only black mark on a white cross. The family I was living with never forgave me."

She came to expect rebuffs or the indifference of a new guardian, who, on the first day of school, took her to the door and pointed: "Go down two blocks, turn left and keep going till you see the school." She got used to being left in neighborhood movie theaters on endless Saturday afternoons, seeing the movie over and over until long past her bedtime. It required no special clairvoyance on her part to understand that her successive "parents" cared little about her. Once she remembered passing a closed door and hearing a woman say, "I've got to get rid of that quiet little girl, she makes me nervous." As her childish efforts to win love and acceptance were repeatedly rejected, she gradually withdrew into the world of fantasy.

She invented solitary games. Once, as a Christmas present, she asked for a flashlight. With this as a prop, Marilyn for weeks afterward played detective, prowling up and down the nearby streets in full daylight intently jotting down the numbers of license plates. On the way to school she composed lengthy fantasies, and even in the classroom spent much of her time dreaming about an imaginary father who was kind and good and looked like Clark Gable.

Once, when no family could be found to take her, Norma Jean stayed for several months at the Los Angeles Orphans' Home Society, a temporary refuge for children from broken families. She tried to run away, but was caught and taken before the superintendent. She stood there rigid and silent, awaiting her punishment. Instead, the superintendent remarked how pretty Norma Jean looked. Taking out her own powder puff, she gently patted it across the youngster's shiny nose. The little girl looked up, baffled by this unexpected kindness.

"No one ever before had noticed my hair, or my face—or even me—I guess," says Marilyn of the occasion. "For the first time in my life, I felt loved."

She soon moved on to another foster home, however. As she grew older, Norma Jean became tall and gawky, with short straw-like hair, hesitant, sometimes stuttering speech, and a shy, scared manner. One family called her "little mouse," and the only way in which boys noticed her was to sing out "Norma Jean—string bean."

A HOME WITH MOTHERLY CARE

At about the time she entered junior high school at the age of twelve, Norma Jean underwent a startling physical change. She began to fill out. The change in the attitude of the boys was no less startling. Their gibes changed to whistles. In the same year she moved to West Los Angeles, where, in the home of a childless widow, Mrs. Ana Lower, Norma Jean found for the first time the warmth and maternal affection she had never had.

When boys would walk Norma Jean home from school, "Aunt Ana" would invite them in for a cold lemonade. When a crush on a neighboring twenty-five-year-old aircraft worker received no response, Aunt Ana compassionately understood. And when they could afford only one change of school clothes, Aunt Ana would wash and iron every day so the girl at least could be clean and fresh.

Norma Jean began to blossom. At school she developed a hero worship for Abraham Lincoln and spent hours at home doing unrequired extra work. She even won a prize for writing a short story, which the teacher said was the best he ever had received from a student. Her work was so good that she skipped a grade, the high seventh.

After two years, Aunt Ana's job began to take her away from home much of the time, and it again became necessary for Norma Jean to move on. Nonetheless, she made frequent trips back to the West Los Angeles home until Aunt Ana's death three years ago. Today, Marilyn still remembers Mrs. Lower with the attachment most children feel for their real mothers.

At sixteen, when her twelfth set of foster parents prepared to send her to another home because of a trip East, Marilyn impetuously married a twenty-three-year-old boyfriend in the merchant marine. The hasty marriage soon broke up, and Marilyn found herself compelled to earn a living.

With no training for any career, she turned to modeling. She stayed at it for a couple of years, and by the summer of 1946, her appearance on several magazine covers had brought talent scouts from both Howard Hughes and Fox studios in her pursuit. Suddenly, things happened fast. Within a matter of days, she had been tested at Fox, been signed to a contract beginning at $125 a week, and had had her name changed to Marilyn Monroe.

FROM A CAMERAMAN'S ANGLE

"When I first watched her," says Leon Shamroy, the Academy Award-winning cameraman who made the screen test, "I thought: This girl will be another Harlow—and I still do. Her natural beauty plus her inferiority complex gave her a look of mystery."

Marilyn was rushed into a small role in a Technicolor film called *Scudda Hoo! Scudda Hay!*, but her part failed to survive the economies of the cutting room. During the next few months, while she gradually lost some of her shyness posing for pinups, Marilyn had only one other opportunity to gain an audience. One March day the publicity department set up a shot in which she posed clad in a flesh-colored negligee. Afterward she had to walk a quarter mile back to the wardrobe department to get her clothes, and a strong wind had arisen as she strolled up the company street past the administration building. Word of what was happening passed around like lightning.

"It was like the Lindbergh homecoming," recalls a studio executive. "People were leaning out of every window. And there was Marilyn, naive and completely unperturbed, smiling and waving up at everybody she knew, didn't know or hoped to know."

Unfortunately, the one executive who missed the display was Zanuck. Soon thereafter, still not having met Miss Monroe and apparently unaware of her charms, he failed to pick up her option at the end of her first year, and Marilyn returned to the limbo of forgotten Hollywood Blondes.

Signed on at Columbia a few months later, she was given a role as a burlesque queen in *Ladies of the Chorus*, a B picture made in nine days, which few people saw and even fewer remember. Her only other appearance in a six-month stay at Columbia was on the wall of a Western set, as a pinup serenaded by Gene Autry.

The first time most people in Hollywood recall seeing Marilyn Monroe on the screen was in an eight-word part in the Marx Brothers comedy *Love Happy*, made for United Artists shortly after she left Columbia. The scene called for Marilyn to walk into an office dressed in a tight-fitting, silver lame evening gown and anxiously tell private eye Groucho Marx, "I need your help." Groucho was then to set up the gag with an innocent, "What can I do?" Whereupon Marilyn was to hip-wiggle out of the door, replying, "Men keep following me."

When they started shooting, Marilyn sashayed into the room with the impact of a fifty-piece brass band. Groucho stared, said his line, "What can I do for you?" as scheduled. Then suddenly he turned to face the camera, raised his famous eyebrows and ad-libbed, "Am I kidding?"

So effective was Marilyn Monroe's brief appearance that she was featured in all the advertising and sent on a personal appearance tour to exploit the picture.

Aside from these short-term chores, Marilyn lived a hand-to-mouth existence. Once, after several good modeling jobs, she bought a small convertible, but lost it quickly to the finance company. At another time, dead broke, she found sanctuary and a helping hand in the home of Lucille Ryman, talent department head at M-G-M. Another friend, and a top Hollywood agent, the late Johnny Hyde, tried to help her career along. But a short stint as a dancing girl in the Fox Western, *Ticket to Tomahawk*, merely paid off old grocery bills.

It was not until early last year that Marilyn got her first big break, when Miss Ryman recommended her to John Huston for a role in *The Asphalt Jungle*. Despite his doubts as to her acting ability, Huston promised her a tryout. After working with her coach, Natasha Lytess, for three days, Marilyn returned and read through the scene for the director. Before he could say a word, she asked: "Please, Mr. Huston, let me do it again? I know I can do better."

When Huston nodded assent, Marilyn got out of the stiff-backed chair, kicked off her high-heeled shoes, and sat cross-legged on the floor, to read the part with childlike ease. She got the role.

Before its public release, Fox director Joe Mankiewicz saw *The Asphalt Jungle* at a private screening and decided Miss Monroe looked like the type he needed for the dumb blonde in *All About Eve*. She got the part, of course, and did well with it. That was her second big break, and it led directly to the third, and biggest yet.

After Zanuck saw the first day's rushes on *All About Eve*, he put in a hasty call for Miss Monroe and her agent. Slightly embarrassed when Marilyn told him she had tried without success to see him while working for Fox three years previously, Zanuck made up for it with a new seven-year contract that started at $500 a week, with options up to $3,500 a week. Marilyn, at long last, had her foot firmly planted on the ladder.

Off the screen, Marilyn Monroe has managed to maintain an almost Garbo-like secrecy about her private life. At the studio, she makes friends easily and is well liked, but her only really close personal friends are Natasha Lytess and Lucille Ryman. She is rarely seen at nightclubs, and her refusal to follow the approved starlet custom of being seen with as many different men as often as possible has puzzled even the usually clairvoyant columnists. Their bewilderment, in turn, puzzles her. "If there were someone I was really interested in, I'd go out with him all I could. But why go out on dates just to be going out?"

Marilyn doesn't even show up at formal premieres, normally considered compulsory attendance affairs for starlets. When the publicity department demanded that she make an appearance at the premiere of *All About Eve*, she flatly refused, explaining that she had to study her lines for a screen test the following morning.

But at the studio and in her public appearances Marilyn eagerly fulfills all the requirements expected of a starlet. She is particularly concerned with looking her best, and spends hours at the makeup table in preparation for even commonplace engagements. The people at Fox who are responsible for seeing that she gets to appointments on time are certain that if each day had thirty hours, Marilyn would use them all in getting ready. No matter how much advance notice she is given, she is always late. Her "I'll be just a minute" can range anywhere from twenty minutes to two hours.

Actually this concern stems from her childhood eagerness to please. For in her unguarded moments, Marilyn is still a shy, uncertain girl, who takes solitary pleasure in long early-morning walks up and down the vacant Beverly Hills alleys, clad in old shirts and faded blue jeans. She has an oppressive awareness of the swift passage of time and of her own perishability. She works long hours at home over her lines; beside her is a large wall mirror—waxed so that her own image will not distract her. On the mirror is scrawled the one Latin word she knows—*nunc*—meaning now.

"I'm twenty-three now," said Marilyn recently, in the tone of someone who has discovered she has an incurable ailment. "Soon I'll be twenty-five. Before I know it, I'll be twenty-eight."

Marilyn lives in a small Beverly Hills apartment, with few of the fairy princess trappings that she once dreamed about and can now afford. Her wardrobe is modest, and the most notable furnishings are an exercise board, a phonograph with records ranging from Beethoven to Jelly Roll Morton, and a multitude of books.

In the past, it has been standard operating procedure for some press agents to suggest that the harebrained cuties they publicize are really fourteen-carat intellects who furrow their brows nightly over Albert Schweitzer, Leo Tolstoy and Ralph Waldo Emerson. The astonishing fact is that Marilyn does just that—not because she is an old friend of those writers, but because she would like to be. On a shelf over her bed and in her three-tier bookcase is an impressive array of well-thumbed volumes by such people as Walt Whitman, Rainer Maria Rilke, John Milton, and Lincoln Steffens (plus Schweitzer, Tolstoy, and Emerson).

Without any hullabaloo, Marilyn quietly enrolled last fall at the University of California's night school in downtown Los Angeles for a course in "Backgrounds of Literature." She appeared at the sessions without makeup and in informal jacket and skirt, and it was several weeks before anyone in the course knew that "Miss Monroe" was in the movies. When Marilyn was absent one night, a student brought to class a

movie magazine with her picture in it. At first the teacher,
Claire Seay, refused to believe it. "Marilyn was so attentive,
so modest and so humble that she could have been some girl
who had just come from a convent," Mrs. Seay said later.

Aside from the two-year period when she was with Aunt
Ana, Marilyn never paid much attention to her studies. Today
she has an insatiable desire to make up for it, to learn new
things. At night school she is constantly pestering the student
next to her to find out what certain big words mean. Quite
often, like other pretty actresses, she finds herself at parties
among famous people like William Saroyan, California's Gov-
ernor Earl Warren, or Irving Berlin. When the conversation
switches to topics like the use of the veto in the United Nations,
Marilyn becomes the most attentive listener. The next day she
is likely to go to a bookstore for a volume on the subject.

DRAB CHILDHOOD SEEN AS ASSET

Marilyn has long since resigned herself to the fact that when-
ever she tries to explain her genuine interest in new subjects
or ideas she runs into a wall of disbelief. This problem is well
understood by her coach: Natasha Lytess feels that Marilyn's
unhappy childhood may one day help her to become an actress of unexpected depth.

"There's more to Marilyn than meets the eye," says Miss
Lytess. "The trouble is that when people look at her they immediately figure her as a typical Hollywood Blonde. It's not
their fault, though. Marilyn's soul just doesn't fit her body."

Understandably, after being around Hollywood for five

years, Marilyn is impatient to prove herself in something more than supporting parts. At Fox, where they are building her up gradually, she has just completed her biggest role yet, assisting Claudette Colbert and MacDonald Carey in *Let's Make It Legal*, scheduled for November release. The Monroe glamor gets full display in this film: she appears in two varieties of swimming suits, one brief tennis costume, a sweater-tight golf outfit, two slinky cocktail dresses and one low-cut evening gown.

Other studios, realizing what even one minute of Monroe can do for the box office, have requested her for parts in their forthcoming productions. Most persistent has been RKO, which wanted Marilyn for the lead in *High Heels*, a story of a dance-hall hostess. But so far 20th Century-Fox has refused all loan-out requests.

Meanwhile, like Topsy, who "just growed," Marilyn believes in letting her curiosity lead her. After the innumerable parental restrictions of her childhood she cannot bear the sense of being cramped by authority or set patterns.

Perhaps that explains what she means when she says, "Someday I want to have a house of my own with trees and grass and hedges all around, but never trim them at all—just let them grow any old way they want."

QUIZZING
MARILYN MONROE

INTERVIEW BY HELEN HOVER
MOTION PICTURE MAGAZINE
JANUARY 1954

The following interview appeared in Motion Picture Magazine *in January 1954. It comprises questions sent in by readers to Helen Hover, who then "quizzed" Marilyn.*

HELEN HOVER: Is it true you dress for men?

MARILYN MONROE: Don't most women dress for men? Isn't it true that men and women have mutual appreciation of each other?

HOVER: Why do you wear low cut gowns?

MONROE: I haven't really noticed.

HOVER: What do you do in your spare time?

MONROE: When an actress is building her career in pictures, as I am, there is very little spare time. What little there is I spend in reading and studying.

HOVER: In *Niagara*, were you clad only in a sheet when you were lying in bed, or were you wearing other clothes underneath?

MONROE: I always wear clothes appropriate to the occasion.

HOVER: What is your description of the ideal man?

MONROE: Someone who is gentle and considerate—but I've never thought of one "ideal man." I doubt if there is such a person.

HOVER: How do you feel about being the sexiest girl in Hollywood?

MONROE: Isn't that a "loaded question"?

HOVER: What do you do to keep your body so beautiful?

MONROE: I walk, exercise, and study body control.

HOVER: What do you think of girls in pictures who try to imitate you?

MONROE: This is a free and democratic country and no one has a monopoly on anything.

HOVER: What is your age, birthplace, and nationality?

MONROE: I was born in Los Angeles on June 1st. I'm an American.

HOVER: How many different boyfriends do you have a week?

MONROE: I think you've been reading too many gossip columns.

HOVER: Are you happy being the type you are, or would you rather be more like Ann Blyth or Jeanne Crain?

MONROE: I am content to be Marilyn Monroe, to the best of my ability. Being oneself is a twenty-four-hour-a-day job anyway, isn't it?

HOVER: What is your worst fault?

MONROE: I probably have many, but my worst is my difficulty in remembering that there are only sixty minutes in an hour. I'm invariably late, but I can't break myself of it.

HOVER: Do you like to dress up and go out at night to formal affairs?

MONROE: No. I don't go to many formal affairs, and when I do I usually go by myself because I want to, or else with someone from the studio. These formal affairs are in the line of duty, anyway.

HOVER: Do you think it is rude, or do you like it when men whistle at you?

MONROE: Any girl who resents whistles should live on a desert island.

HOVER: What are your measurements?

MONROE: Bust 37, waist 23.5, hips 37.5—or so they tell me.

HOVER: Is it true that you really posed for calendar pictures?

MONROE: Yes.

HOVER: Do you act the same off screen as you do on?

MONROE: When I work I act; when I'm home I don't act. Do you do the same things at home as when you're working at your job as secretary, salesgirl, teacher, clerk or whatever? Why bring your work home with you?

HOVER: What is your favorite pastime?

MONROE: Walking. I can walk alone for hours and enjoy it.

HOVER: Were you popular at school?

MONROE: I won no popularity awards, but I did have a number of good friends.

HOVER: How many dates do you have a week?

MONROE: When I'm working in a picture I have no time to go out. Besides, I don't think in terms of dates per week, that's silly. If someone asks me to go out, and I find his company enjoyable, I go out with them. If not then I'd rather stay home.

HOVER: If you weren't an actress, what would you want to be?

MONROE: It's funny, but I've never thought of being anything but an actress.

HOVER: Do you walk in real life the way you did in *Niagara*?

MONROE: I never think about the way I walk. But since I was playing a certain type of girl in the picture who was not myself, and since the way I walked helped emphasize her, I walked as I did. I'm sure my real-life walk is not exactly the same.

HOVER: Are you happy with the type of publicity you get or would you rather be known for something else besides your figure?

MONROE: I want to be known as a good actress.

HOVER: Who was your first love?

MONROE: No one you would know.

HOVER: Are you sultry and sexy by nature and do you enjoy being this type?

MONROE: What is a type? I am myself—Marilyn Monroe.

HOVER: What are your favorite hobbies?

MONROE: Swimming, collecting records, reading and dancing, when I have time.

HOVER: What is the truth about your romance with Joe DiMaggio?

MONROE: Mr. DiMaggio is a good friend and a gentleman I greatly admire.

HOVER: Have you a temper, and what makes you lose it?

MONROE: I have a little temper, and I really lose it when people write untruths about me.

HOVER: What attracts you first to a man, his looks or personality?

MONROE: It depends on the man, but I'd say that personality means more. However, a sense of humor is a wonderful help as far as I'm concerned in sizing up a man's personality.

HOVER: Who is your best girlfriend?

MONROE: I don't have a best girlfriend, but I do have many good friends whose companionship is worth much to me.

HOVER: Was there friction between you and Jane Russell when you were making *Gentlemen Prefer Blondes*?

MONROE: None whatsoever. I don't know why this rumor sprang up unless people just can't believe that two women can work together in harmony. I consider Jane to be one of the sweetest persons I've ever met, and I'm happy to call her my friend.

HOVER: What's your idea of a good time when dating?

MONROE: I like a quiet evening with someone whose personality and conversation intrigues me.

HOVER: How do you feel about criticism of your low-cut gowns?

MONROE: I don't like unfair criticism at any time. Do you? I feel that some of the criticism has been unfair.

HOVER: What kind of man do you want to marry?

MONROE: How can I say? I'm not thinking of marrying at the moment. I do want to get married and have children someday, that's for sure, but I'll cross the career-marriage bridge when I get to it.

HOVER: What kind of life did you live before you became a star?

MONROE: There were some difficult days and some pleasant ones. I went to school, held down a number of jobs, looked for openings in pictures all the time, had many disappointments which were very crushing and finally reached some small measure of success.

HOVER: Do you ever want to play something besides a siren on the screen?

MONROE: Certainly. I want to play a variety of roles. I don't think it's good to be typed.

THE NEW MARILYN MONROE

CONVERSATION WITH PETE MARTIN
THE SATURDAY EVENING POST
MAY 5, 1956

I said to Marilyn Monroe, "Pictures of you usually show you with mouth open and your eyes half closed. Did some photographer sell you the idea that having your picture taken that way makes you look sexier?"

She replied in what I'd come to recognize as pure Monroese. "The formation of my lids must make them look heavy or else I'm thinking of something," she told me. "Sometimes I'm thinking of men. Other times I'm thinking of some man in particular. It's easier to look sexy when you're thinking of some man in particular. As for my mouth being open all the time, I even sleep with it open. I know, because it's open when I wake up. I never consciously think of my mouth, but I do consciously think about what I'm thinking about."

Tucked away in that paragraph like blueberries in a hot muffin were several genuine Monroeisms. I had studied the subject long enough to be able to tell a genuine Monroeism from a spurious one.

When I asked her, "Has anyone ever accused you of wearing falsies?" she came through with a genuine Monroeism.

"Yes," she told me, her eyes flashing indignantly.

"Naturally," she went on, "it was another actress who accused me. My answer to that is, quote: Those who know me better know better. That's all. Unquote."

Another Monroeism followed hard on the heels of that. I said, "I've heard that you wowed the marines in Korea when you climbed up onto a platform to say a few words to them, and they whistled at you and made wolf calls."

"I know the time you're talking about," she said. "It wasn't in Korea at all; it was at Camp Pendleton, California. They wanted me to say a few words, so I said, 'You fellows down there are always whistling at sweater girls. Well, take away their sweaters and what have you got?' For some reason they screamed and yelled."

Another example came forth when Marilyn was asked if she and the playwright, Arthur Miller, were having an affair. "How can they say we're having a romance?" she replied. "He's married."

Still another Monroeism had emerged from a press conference in the Plaza Hotel, in New York City. It was held to announce her teaming with Sir Laurence Olivier in an acting-directing-producing venture—a get-together described by one of those present as "one of the least likely duos in cinematic history." The big Monroeism of that occasion was Marilyn's answer to the query, "Miss Monroe, do you still want to do *The Brothers Karamazov* on Broadway?"

"I don't want to play The Brothers," she said. "I want to play Grushenka from that book. She's a girl."

Listening to her as she talked to me now, I thought, nobody can write dialogue for her which could possibly sound half as much like her as the dialogue she thinks up for herself.

Nunnally Johnson, who produced the film *How to Marry a Millionaire*, costarring Marilyn, told me, "When I talked to her when she first came on the lot, I felt as if I were talking to a girl under water. I couldn't tell whether I was getting through to her or not. She lived behind a fuzz curtain."

Johnson also directed *How to be Very, Very Popular*, and when Sheree North took Marilyn's place in that film, he announced: "Sheree will not use the Monroe technique in *How to be Very, Very Popular*. She will play the entire role with her mouth closed."

Marilyn's last sentence to me, "I never consciously think of my mouth, but I do consciously think about what I'm thinking about," seemed a trifle murky, but I had no time to work on it, for, without pausing, she said, "Another writer asked me, 'What do you think of sex?' and I told him, 'It's a part of nature. I go along with nature.' Zsa Zsa Gabor was supposed to write an article for a magazine on the subject: 'What's Wrong with American Men,' and I did marginal notes for it. The editor cut out my best lines. I wrote, 'If there's anything wrong with the way American men look at sex, it's not their fault. After all, they're descended from the Puritans, who got off the boat on the wrong foot—or was it the Pilgrims?—and there's still a lot of that puritanical stuff around.' The editor didn't use that one."

I carefully wrote down every word she said to me. She told me that she'd rather I wouldn't use a tape-recording machine while interviewing her. "It would make me nervous to see that thing going round and round," she insisted. So I used pencils and a notebook instead. But I didn't use them right away.

I had to wait for her to walk from her bedroom into the living room of her apartment, where I sat ready to talk to her. It took her an hour and a half to make that journey. At 3:45, Lois Weber, the pleasant young woman who handled the Monroe New York publicity, admitted me to the apartment Marilyn was occupying. She pushed the buzzer outside of a door on the eighth floor of an apartment building on Sutton Place South, and a voice asked, "Who is it?"

"It's me," said my chaperone.

The lock clickety-clicked open, but when we went in, Marilyn was nowhere in sight. She had retreated into a bedroom. Her voice said to us through the door, "I'll be out in just seven minutes."

A publicity man to whom I'd talked at Marilyn's studio in Hollywood had warned me, "She'll stand you up a couple of times before you meet her. Then she'll be late, and when I say late, I mean real late. You'll be so burned at her before she walks in that you'll wrap up your little voice-recording machine and get ready to leave at least three times—maybe four times—before she shows. But somebody will persuade you to wait, and finally Marilyn will come in, and before you know it, she'll have you wrapped up too. For she's warmhearted, amusing, and likable, even if her lateness is a pain in the neck. And after that, if somebody says, 'That was mighty thoughtless of old Marilyn, keeping you waiting like that,' you'll want to slug him for being mean.

"What you won't know," that studio publicity man went on, "is that while you're having hell's own headache waiting for her, whatever publicity worker is trying to get her to see you is having an even bigger headache. Marilyn will be telling that publicity worker that her stomach is so upset that she's been throwing up for hours; she hasn't been able to get her makeup on right; or that she's got a bum deal in the wardrobe department and hasn't anything to wear."

So, in an effort to be witty, when Marilyn said, through the closed door, "I'll be out in just seven minutes," I said, "I'll settle for eight." Time was to prove it the unfunniest remark I've ever made. One hour later I asked Lois Weber, "What do you suppose she's doing in there?"

"You know how it is," my publicity-girl chaperone said soothingly, "a girl has to put on her face."

"What has she got, two heads?" I asked politely. A half hour later I suggested that Lois Weber go into the next room and see what was causing the delay.

Waiting for Lois Weber, I roamed the apartment. On a table lay a play manuscript. Typed on its cover was: *Fallen Angels*, by Noel Coward. Among the books which seemed in current use were Bernard Shaw's *Letters to Ellen Terry*, Shaw's *Letters to Mrs. Patrick Campbell*, *Gertrude Lawrence as Mrs. A.*, by Richard Aldrich.

Mute evidence of Marilyn's widely publicized drama studies at the Actors Studio, where she was said to be seeking out the secrets of artistic acting, was a copy of James Joyce's *Ulysses*. Several lines of dialogue from that volume had been penciled on a piece of paper, obviously to be recited by or to a group of drama students; then the piece of paper had been thrust part way into the book. Lying on the floor was a large recording of John Barrymore as Hamlet.

That dialogue from *Ulysses* and the Barrymore recording represented one of the reasons why I was there. I'd read that Marilyn had gone "long hair" and "art theaterish," and I wanted to see for myself. Just seeing it in print didn't make it true.

Millions of words had been written about the alluring blonde in whose living room I sat, but most of those words had been of the "authorized" or "with-Marilyn's-blessing" variety. Several millions of them had appeared in fan magazines—after having first been OK'd by the 20th Century-Fox publicity department.

I'd read a lot of those words, but I still felt that I didn't understand this dame and I was sure that a lot of other people felt the same way about her and that, like myself, they'd been asking themselves for years, "What's she really like?"

On top of that, they were probably asking themselves other questions—as I was doing. "Why did she blow her marriage with Joe DiMaggio? Why did she walk out on a movie career which was paying her heavy money? Why did she duck California in favor of New York? Why, after she holed up there, did she attend the art-for-art's-sake Actors Studio—surely an unlikely place for a girl who, up to that time, had done most of her acting with her hips?"

I hoped that when I talked to her she would tell me the answers to some of these things. Maybe I'd even see the "new Marilyn Monroe" I'd heard existed.

Lois Weber came back to report: "She thinks the maid must have gone off with the top of her tapered slacks. She's running around without a top on."

In an effort to keep me from brooding, Lois Weber said, "The azalea people down in Wilmington, North Carolina, want her for a personal appearance in April, but I told them they'd have to call me in April. Who knows where she'll be then?"

The minutes crawled by and I thought of various things that people had told me about Marilyn before I'd begun my marathon wait in her Sutton Place apartment. Every male friend I had told I was doing a story about Marilyn had asked me, "Can I go along to hold your notebook?" or "You call *that* work?" or "You get *paid* for that?" or "Can't I go along and hold the flash bulbs?" Apparently they felt that if they failed to go into a blood-bubbling, he-man routine at the drop of her name, their maleness was suspect. When Marilyn appeared breathless and friendly as a puppy, I told her of this phenomenon. "How do you explain it?" I asked. "Have you become a symbol of sex?"

She gave my query thought before answering. "There are people to whom other people react, and other people who do nothing for people," she said. "I react to men, too, but I don't do it because I'm trying to prove I'm a woman. Personally I react to Marlon Brando. He's a favorite of mine. There are two kinds of reactions. When you see some people you say, 'Gee!' When you see other people you say, 'Ugh!' If that part about my being a symbol of sex is true, it ought to help at the box office, but I don't want to be too commercial about it." Quite seriously she said, "After all, it's a responsibility, too—being a symbol, I mean."

I told her I'd heard that among the titles bestowed upon her were Woo-Woo Girl, Miss Cheesecake, The Girl with the Horizontal Walk. "I don't get what they mean by 'horizontal

walk,'" she said. "Naturally I know what walking means—
anybody knows that—and horizontal means not vertical.
So what?" I thought of trying to blueprint it for her; then
decided not to.

The Hollywood publicity worker who had warned me
that she would be "real late" had talked to me quite frankly
about Marilyn; he had pulled no punches; but since it is unfair to quote a publicity worker by name, I'll call him Jones.
And since "flack" is Hollywood slang for publicity man, I'll
call him Flack Jones.

Jones worked for 20th Century-Fox during the years before Marilyn staged her walkout. Since then he has moved
on to bigger—if not better—things. He has opened his own
public-relations office, with branches in Paris and Rome. He
is bald as a peeled egg. He is as broad as a small barn door;
a junior-executive-sized Mister Five-by-Five. He wears black-
rimmed glasses instead of the clear tortoise-shell plastic variety.

"A thing that fascinates me is this," I told Flack Jones:
"The first time I ever saw her I was sitting with a friend in the
Fox commissary and this girl came in without any makeup
on. She was wearing a blouse and skirt, and she sat against
the wall. She bore no resemblance to anybody I'd ever seen
before, but, to my amazement, my friend said, 'That's Marilyn Monroe.' What I want to know is: Does she have to get
into her Marilyn Monroe suit or put on her Marilyn Monroe
face before she looks like Marilyn Monroe?"

"This is true of all platinum blondes or whatever you
call the highly dyed jobs we have out here," Flack Jones said.
"If their hair isn't touched up and coiffured exactly right; if
they're not gowned perfectly and their makeup is not one

hundred percent, they look gruesome. This is not peculiar to Monroe; it's peculiar to every other synthetic blonde I've ever known in picture business. There are very few natural blondes in Hollywood and, so far as I know, there have been no natural platinum blondes in mankind's history, except albinos. They are strictly a product of the twentieth century. They're created blondes, and when you create a blonde you have to complete your creation with makeup and dramatic clothes, otherwise you've got only part of an assembly job."

I also talked to a member of the Fox Studio legal staff, who told me a Monroe story I found provocative. "One day," he said, "she was in this office, and I said to her, 'It would be better for you to sign this contract this year instead of next. It will save you money.' She looked at me and said, 'I'm not interested in money. I just want to be wonderful.' Then she walked out." The legal light looked at me helplessly and shrugged. "What do you suppose she meant by that?" he asked. I said I had no idea, but that I'd try to find out.

And I asked a friend high enough up in the Fox hierarchy to know the answer. "Why do you think your studio let her come back to work for it after she walked out and stayed in New York for fifteen months?"

"Our attitude was that she'd never work on our lot again," he announced firmly; then he grinned, "Unless we needed her."

One of my longer talks was with Billy Wilder, who directed her in the film *The Seven Year Itch*.

"What do you want to know?" he asked when I went to see him in his Beverly Hills home.

"One of the interesting things about this Monroe girl, to me," I said, "is she seemed in danger of spoiling what had begun as a successful career by running away from it. I began to ask myself: How long can a movie actress afford to stay away from moviemaking and still remain a star? The mere strangeness of her staying away gets her terrific press for a while and makes everyone in the country conscious of her, but is it possible to stay away so long that you're forgotten? Was that about to happen to Marilyn?"

"I don't think there was any danger of Marilyn sinking into oblivion," Wilder said. "A thing like her doesn't come along every minute."

I asked, "What do you mean 'a thing like her?'"

"She has what I call flesh impact," he told me. "It's very rare. Three I remember are Clara Bow, Jean Harlow and Rita Hayworth. Such girls have flesh which photographs like flesh. You feel you can reach out and touch it."

"I've heard that it's a moot question as to whether Marilyn's an actress or not," I said.

"I've heard that, too," he replied. "Before we go further I must tell you that I like the girl, but it's also moot whether you have to be an actor or an actress to be a success in pictures. I'm sure you've heard the theory that there are two kinds of stars—those who can act and those who are personalities. I'll take a personality any time. Something comes down from the screen to you when you see them, in a way that it doesn't always come from the indifferently paid actors, although they may be perfect at their jobs."

"It's nothing against them or for them," Flack Jones said, when I repeated Wilder's idea to him. "It's the way this business is put together. If the public likes a personality, he or she goes over. You take Tab Rock," he said (only Tab Rock is not the name he used). "Old Tab's a terrific personality. I doubt if he's ever made a flop picture, but he's never made a really good picture. This fellow can't pick up his hat without instruction, yet he's always picking up villains and throwing them across a bar singlehanded. He can clean up any barroom on the frontier, but he can't clean up a kitchen. He's a nice guy, but no one has ever called him an actor. You take Lloyd Nolan now, or Van Heflin. That's acting for you. You believe them. There are lights and shades and meaning to what they do. But when old Tab Rock comes on the screen, he's got to throw somebody around to prove his art. He can do this quicker than anybody in Hollywood, and this is his great value."

"He sounds brave," I said.

"No one is braver or more scornful about it," Flack Jones said. "His bravery is without parallel in the industry. He's the only man I ever saw who could take a forty-five and go to the Near East [Middle East] and clean the whole mess up in a day or two. He never fails. That's the difference between a personality and an actor."

When I talked to Wilder I said that I'd read that when Marilyn had announced that she wanted to appear in a movie version of *The Brothers Karamazov*, some people hooted.

"The hooters were wrong," Wilder told me. "She meant that she wanted to play the part of Grushenka in that book, and people who haven't read the book don't know that Grushenka is a sex pot. People think this is a long-hair, very thick, very literary book, but Dostoevsky knew what he was doing and there is nothing long-hair about Grushenka. Marilyn knows what she's doing too. She would be a good Grushenka.

"It was after she said that she wanted to be in *The Brothers Karamazov*," Wilder went on, "that she started going to the Actors Studio School of Dramatic Arts in New York. She didn't do it for publicity. She's sincerely trying to improve herself, and I think she should be admired for that. She could have sat here in Hollywood on her pretty little fanny and collected all of the money any ordinary actress would ever want, but she keeps trying.

"Right now, as of today, no matter what she thinks, Marilyn's great value is as a personality, not as an actress. [Wilder told me these things while Marilyn was still in New York being groomed by the Actors Studio. It may be that what happened to her during her eastern schooling in new dramatic ways may change his opinion, but I haven't talked to him since her return to Hollywood.] If she sets out to be artistic and dedicated, and she carries it so far that she's willing to wear Sloppy-Joe sweaters and go without makeup and let her hair hang straight as a string, this is not what has made her great to date. I don't say that it's beyond the realm of possibility that she can establish herself as a straight dramatic actress—it is possible—but it will be another career for her, a starting all over."

Back in New York, when Marilyn made that long, long journey from her bedroom to her living room in her apartment, I said to her, "I've heard your childhood referred to as 'the perfect Cinderella story.'"

"I don't know where they got that," she told me. "I haven't ended up with a prince, and I've never had even one fairy godmother. My birth certificate reads Norma Jean Mortenson. I was told that my father was killed in an automobile accident before I was born, so that is what I've always told people. There was no way I could check on that because my mother was put into a mental institution when I was little, and I was brought up as an orphan."

I had read that she spent her childhood being farmed out to foster parents and to orphanages, but, talking to her, I discovered that there'd been only one orphanage, although it was true about the foster parents. "I have had eleven or twelve sets of them," she told me, "but I don't want to count them all again, to see whether there were eleven or twelve. I hope you won't ask me to. It depresses me. Some families would keep me longer; others would get tired of me in a short time. I must have made them nervous or something."

She thought of something else. "I had one pair of foster parents who, when I was about ten, made me promise never to drink when I grew up, and I signed a pledge never to smoke or swear. My next foster family gave me empty whisky bottles for playthings. With them I played store. I guess I must have had the finest collection of empty whisky bottles any girl ever had. I'd line them up on a plank beside the road, and when people drove along I'd say, 'Wouldn't you like some whisky?' I remember some of the people in the cars driving past my 'whisky' store saying, 'Imagine! Why, it's terrible!' Looking back, I guess I used to playact all the time. For one thing, it meant I could live in a more interesting world than the one around me.

"The first family I lived with told me I couldn't go to the movies because it was sinful," Marilyn said. "I listened to them say the world was coming to an end, and if I was doing something sinful when it happened, I'd go down below,

below, below. So the few times I was able to sneak into a movie, I spent most of the time that I was there praying that the world wouldn't end."

Apparently I had been misinformed about her first marriage, to a young man named Jim Dougherty. I'd got the idea that she'd married him while they were both in Van Nuys High School; that she'd got a "crush" on him because he was president of the student body there, and a big wheel around school.

"That's not true," she told me. "In the first place, he was twenty-one or twenty-two—well, at least he was twenty-one and already out of high school. So all I can say is that he must have been pretty dumb if he were still in high school when I married him. And I didn't have a crush on him, although he claimed I did in a story he wrote about us. The truth is the people I was staying with moved East. They couldn't afford to take me because when they left California they'd stop getting the twenty dollars a month the county or the state was paying them to help them clothe and feed me. So instead of going back into a boarding home or with still another set of foster parents, I got married.

"That marriage ended in a divorce, but not until World War Two was over. Jim is now a policeman. He lives in Reseda, in the San Fernando Valley, and he is happily married and has three daughters. But while he was away in the merchant marines I worked in the dope room of a plane factory. That company not only made planes, it made parachutes.

"For a while I'd been inspecting parachutes. Then they quit letting us girls do that and they had the parachutes inspected on the outside, but I don't think it was because of my inspecting. Then I was in the dope room spraying dope on fuselages. Dope is liquid stuff, like banana oil and glue mixed.

"I was out on sick leave for a few days, and when I came back the army photographers from the Hal Roach Studios, where they had the army photographic headquarters, were around taking photographs and snapping and shooting while I was doping those ships. The army guys saw me and asked, 'Where have you been?'

"'I've been on sick leave,' I said. 'Come outside,' they told me. 'We're going to take your picture.'

"'Can't,' I said. 'The other ladies here in the dope room will give me trouble if I stop doing what I'm doing and go out with you.' That didn't discourage those army photographers. They got special permission for me to go outside from Mr. Whosis, the president of the plant. For a while they posed me rolling ships; then they asked me, 'Don't you have a sweater?'

"'Yes,' I told them, 'it so happens I brought one with me. It's in my locker.' After that I rolled ships around in a sweater. The name of one of those army photographers was David Conover. He lives up near the Canadian border. He kept telling me, 'You should be a model,' but I thought he was flirting. Several weeks later, he brought the color shots he'd taken of me, and he said the Eastman Kodak Company had asked him, 'Who's your model, for goodness' sake?'

"So I began to think that maybe he wasn't kidding about how I ought to be a model. Then I found that a girl could make five dollars an hour modeling, which was different from working ten hours a day for the kind of money I'd been making at the plane plant. And it was a long way from the orphanage, where I'd been paid five cents a week for working in the dining room or ten cents a month for working in the pantry. And out of those big sums a penny every Sunday had to go into the church collection. I never could figure why they took a penny from an orphan for that."

"How did you happen to sign your first movie contract?" I asked.

She tossed a cascade of white-blond tresses from her right eye and said, "I had appeared on five magazine covers. Mostly men's magazines."

What, I asked, did she mean by men's magazines? "Magazines," she said, "with cover girls who are not flat-chested. I was on *See* four or five months in a row. Each time they changed my name. One month I was Norma Jean Dougherty—that was my first husband's name. The second month I was Jean Norman. I don't know what all names they used, but I must have looked different each time. There were different poses— outdoors, indoors, but mostly just sitting looking over the Pacific. You looked at those pictures and you didn't see much ocean, but you saw a lot of me.

"One of the magazines I was on wasn't a man's magazine at all. It was called *Family Circle*. You buy it in supermarkets. I was holding a lamb with a pinafore. I was the one with the pinafore. But on most covers I had on things like a striped towel. The towel was striped because the cover was to be in color and the stripes were the color, and there was a big fan blowing on the towel and on my hair. That was right after my first divorce, and I needed to earn a living bad. I couldn't type. I didn't know how to do anything. So Howard Hughes had an accident."

I wondered if I'd missed something, but apparently I hadn't. "He was in the hospital," she went on, "and Hedda Hopper wrote in her column: 'Howard Hughes must be recuperating because he sent out for photographs of a new girl he's seen on five different magazines.' Right after that Howard Hughes's casting director got my telephone number somehow, and he got in touch with me and he said Howard Hughes wanted to see me.

"But he must have forgotten or changed his mind or something," she said, "because instead of going to see him, I went over to the Fox Studio with a fellow named Harry Lipton, who handled my photography modeling. Expensive cars used to drive up beside me when I was on a street corner or walking on a sidewalk, and the driver would say, 'I could do something for you in pictures. How would you like to be a Goldwyn girl?' I figured those guys in those cars were trying for a pick-up, and I got an agent so I could say to those fellows, 'See my agent.' That's how I happened to be handled by Harry Lipton."

Harry took her to see Ivan Kahn, then head of Fox's talent department, and also to see Ben Lyon, who was doing a talent-scouting job for Fox.

I asked her how it happened that she changed her name from Norma Jean Dougherty to Marilyn Monroe.

"It was Ben Lyon who renamed me," she said. "Ben said that I reminded him of two people, Jean Harlow and somebody else he remembered very well, a girl named Marilyn Miller. When all the talk began about renaming me, I asked them please could I keep my mother's maiden name, which was Monroe; so the choice was whether to call me Jean Monroe or Marilyn Monroe, and Marilyn won."

I asked Flack Jones, "What happened when she came to your studio?"

"She came twice," he said. "The first time was in 1946. We did our best with her, but she just hadn't grown up enough. She was great as far as looks went, but she didn't know how to make the most of her looks—or what to do with them. That came with practice. Not that you have to mature mentally to be a star. In fact, it can be a holdback. It might even defeat you. Stars who are mature mentally are in the minority. But actually we had no stories lying around at that time in which she would appear to advantage. So we tried her out in a picture or two in which she played bit parts—secretaries, the pretty girl in the background. Then we let her go, and she went over to RKO and did a picture with Groucho."

"I didn't see the film," I said, "but you'd think with the Marx Brothers chasing her, like a bosomy mechanical bunny romping about the sound stage a couple of jumps ahead of the greyhounds, the fun would have been fast and furious."

"The trouble was that while the Marx Brothers always chased a dame in their pictures," Flack Jones told me, "they never caught the dame. And usually the dame never became a star, so the whole thing was a waste of time. It was amusing while you were watching it, but the girls usually outran the Marx boys and a career."

Marilyn gave me her own version of Flack Jones's story:

"Most of what I did while I was at Fox that first time was pose for stills. Publicity made up a story about how I was a babysitter who'd been baby-sitting for the casting director and that's how I was discovered. They told me to say that, although it strictly wasn't true. You'd think that they would have used a little more imagination and have had me at least a daddy sitter."

Flack Jones had filled me in on some more Monroe chronology: "After she left us she went to Metro and appeared in *The Asphalt Jungle*, directed by John Huston," he said. "Marilyn's role was small. She was only a walk-on, but she must have looked good to Darryl Zanuck, for when he saw it, he re-signed her. *Asphalt Jungle* was one of those gangster things. There was a crooked legal mouthpiece in it, a suave fellow, played by Louis Calhern. Marilyn was his 'niece'; which was a nice word for 'keptie.' She'd say a few lines of dialogue; then she'd look up at him with those big eyes and call him 'Uncle.'"

"When did you first notice her impact on the public?" I asked.

"Once we got her rolling, it was like a tidal wave," he said. "We began to release some photographs of her, and as soon as they appeared in print, we had requests for more from all over the world. We had the newspapers begging for art; then the photo syndicates wanted her; then the magazines began to drool. For a while we were servicing three or four photos to key newspapers all over the world once a week—and that was before she had appeared in a picture.

"Once this building-up process started," Flack Jones explained, "other people got interested in her. We called up the top cameramen around town who had their own outlets, and we told them what we had, and we asked them if they'd like to photograph her. They said, 'Ho, boy, yes.'

"We told them what the deal was," Flack Jones went on. "We said, 'We think this girl has a great future; she's beautiful, her chassis is great, and are you interested?' Each guy had his own idea of what he wanted, and he let his imagination play upon her. This is the way such things get done. They're not created by one person. They're the creation of all of the press representatives who cover Hollywood for all the publications in the world, which means about three hundred and fifty people.

"Everybody in the studio publicity department worked on her." Jones ticked them off on his fingertips, "The picture division, the magazine division, the fan-magazine division, the planters who plant the columnists, the radio planters, and so forth. Then, when you make a motion picture, a 'unit man' or 'unit woman' is assigned to cover its shooting, and he or she handles publicity for that film alone. In addition, the whole department works on the same picture. Our department is highly specialized, but each specialist makes his contribution to the personality we're erecting in the public's mind."

"I've met a couple of press agents who've been unit men on Marilyn's films," I said.

"But the unit man is not always the same for a certain star's pictures," Jones said. "Sonia Wilson's been unit woman on Monroe pictures, and Frankie Neal's been a unit man on her pictures, but Roy Craft has been her unit man more than anyone else. Roy likes her. He gets along with her fine."

There was something else I wanted to know. "In addition to distributing her photographs," I asked, "did you have her show up at different places where you thought her appearance would do her good?"

"We took her to all of the cocktail parties we thought were important," Flack Jones said. "For instance, one picture magazine had its annual cocktail party, and we told Marilyn she ought to show so we could introduce her to various editors, columnists and radio and TV people. She waited until everybody had arrived; then she came in in this red gown. That gown became famous. She'd had sense enough to buy it a size or two too small, and it had what Joe Hyams calls 'break-away straps.'

"When she came in, everybody stopped doing what they were doing and their eyes went, 'Boing, boing,'" Flack Jones went on. "The publisher of the magazine who was picking up the tab for the party shook hands with her a long, long time. After a while he turned to one of his associate editors and said, 'We ought to have a picture of this little girl in our book.' Then he looked at her again and said, 'Possibly we should have her on the cover.'"

Flack Jones grinned. "So that's the way things went," he said. "Some months there were as many as fifteen or sixteen covers of her on the newsstands at once. She came back to the Fox lot in 1950 to appear in *All About Eve*, but she was not anyone's great, big, brilliant discovery until we got our still cameras focused on her and started spreading those Marilyn Monroe shots all over the universe."

"What did she do in *All About Eve*?" I asked. "I don't remember."

"She's the dumb broad who walks into a party at Bette Davis's place leaning on George Sanders's arm," he said. "There's dialogue which shows you that Sanders is a critic, like George Jean Nathan; and he brings this beautiful dish

Marilyn in, and he sights a producer played by Gregory Ratoff. Sanders points at Ratoff and says to Marilyn, 'There's
a real live producer, honey. Go do yourself some good.' So
Marilyn goes off to do herself some good while Sanders stays
in his own price class with Bette."

"Do you remember the first day she came to work?" I
asked.

"Do I remember?" he said. "She was in an Angora sweater
out to there. While we were shooting her in photography,
the word got around and the boys rushed across the hall to
get an eyeful. Next we did some layouts with her for picture
magazines. We put her in a negligee, and she liked it so much
that she wouldn't take it off. She walked all over the lot in it,
yelling, 'Yoo hoo' at strangers as far away as the third floor
of the administration building. Pretty soon the whole third
floor was looking down at her. The first and second floors
looked too."

Flack Jones did an abrupt shift into the present tense,
"It's a bright, sunny day; the wind is blowing and she has Nature working with her. It has taken Nature quite a while to
bring her to the ripe-peach perfection she reaches on that day,
but it finally makes it. The wind does the rest. She walks all
over the lot, has a ball for herself, and so does everybody else."

Then he shifted back again, "After that we took her to
the beach with a lot of wardrobe changes. But the basic idea
was that this is a beautiful girl with a great body, and that idea
was always the same, although we had different approaches
to it. We had color shots, we had black-and-white shots, we
had mountain shots, we had field shots, faked water-skiing
shots—every type of approach we could think of. Picnicking,

walking—anything a person does, we let her do it. When we began to see what she did best, we concentrated on it.

"Women always hate the obvious in sex," Flack Jones said, "and men love it." Apparently he had given this matter a lot of thought. He had even worked out a philosophy about it. "Guys are instinctively awkward and blundering and naïve— even worldly-wise ones—and subtlety in sex baffles them. Not only that, but they don't have the time. Women who are not supporting a husband have all the time in the world for it. But men have other things to do, like making a dollar; and they like their love-making without preliminaries which last four or five hours. Instinctively Marilyn knows this. She is very down-to-earth, very straightforward."

I asked Marilyn when I talked to her back on Sutton Place, "Do you think men like their sex subtle or fairly obvious?" This was a double check. I already had the male answer.

It seemed to me that she hedged. "Some men prefer subtleties and other men don't want things so subtle," she said. "I don't believe in false modesty. A woman only hurts herself that way. If she's coy she's denying herself an important part of life. Men sometimes believe that you're frigid and cold in the development of a relationship, but if they do, it's not always your fault. Religion has to do with it and how you're brought up. You're stuck with all that."

I remembered something else Wilder had told me before Marilyn's recent return to Hollywood to make the film version of the New York stage hit *Bus Stop*. "You take Monroe, now," he remarked. "Aside from whether she's an actress or not, she's got this lovely little shape, it twitches excitingly, and the public likes to watch it, either coming toward them or going away. There are two schools of thought about her—those who like her and those who attack her—but they both are willing to pay to watch her. Their curiosity is good for eighty cents or a dollar and a quarter or whatever the price of the ticket."

He shook his head thoughtfully. "And she went back East to study at a slow-take arty place, where they feature understatement. Here's a girl who's built herself a career on overstating something, and she's made up her mind to understate. It won't be long before we'll know whether she's right and whether she needs the wardrobe department and the hairdressing department as much as she needs artistic lines to say. It'll be interesting to watch and I hope it works out the way she wants it to, but the lines that the public really wants from her so far are not written in English. They are her curves."

The voice of Flack Jones echoed in the back of my head. "I forgot to tell you. When she finished that Marx Brothers picture, she went over to Columbia for a couple of shows, but she didn't click, and they released her too. After that she was around town for a while going broke. It was then that she posed for that famous nude calendar—the composition of glowing flesh against a red velvet background which threw the public into a tizzy when they learned about it."

I asked Marilyn to tell me the story of that nude calendar herself, and she said, "When the studio first heard about it, everybody there was in a frenzy. They telephoned me on the set where I was working in a quickie called *Don't Bother to Knock*. The person who called asked me, 'What's all this about a calendar of you in the nude? Did you do it?'

"'Yes,' I said. 'Is there anything wrong with it? So they've found out it's me on that calendar. Well, what do you know!'

"'Found out!' he almost screamed. 'There you are, all of you, in full color!' Then he must have gotten mixed up, for first he said, 'Just deny everything'; then he said, 'Don't say anything. I'll be right down.'"

CONVERSATIONS WITH MARILYN

CONVERSATION WITH WILLIAM J. WEATHERBY
CONVERSATIONS WITH MARILYN
1961 [FIRST PUBLISHED IN 1976]

When she was half an hour late, I decided she wasn't coming. Why the hell had she bothered to make the date? But I reminded myself that she had been several hours late on *The Misfits* and that had been more important. How long should I give her? I usually gave people a half hour, but this time I was unwilling to leave after thirty minutes, so I decided to give her an hour.

I had chosen a booth in the back where the lighting was dim, so no one would recognize her and we could talk. It was one of those simple bars with no table service, so I went up to the bar for another drink. If Marilyn was very late, I'd be drunk by the time she got there. But I was convinced by that time she'd either forgotten—the scatterbrained dumb blonde of legend (disappointment was making me nasty)—or she'd decided she couldn't make it on time and so would skip it and make apologies the next time we met at the Actors Studio.

For the first half hour I had kept my eyes on the swinging doors in the distance, but then the bar had become crowded and I'd given up and given all my attention to my drink and my thoughts about an article I was writing about Christopher

Isherwood. I'd interviewed him when I was in Hollywood.

"A dollar for your thoughts," a voice said. A female voice.
A familiar one.

"Not worth it," I said, looking up.

There she was, dressed the same way she had been at the
Actors Studio, except that the head scarf was different and
tied much more loosely. A little of her hair showed. She was
smiling gaily, like someone intent on having a good time. Just
seeing her there certainly made my spirits rise.

I glanced around, a little embarrassed. Maybe a smart
hotel bar was more her style, like the one we'd drunk in in
Reno. "We can go to another bar—"

"No, no, I like it." She sat facing me, grinning. "I'm not
often taken to a *real* bar."

"What'll you have to drink?"

"What are you drinking?"

"Gin and tonic."

"Okay, I'll try that."

I didn't know whether that meant she'd never had one
before, or whether she'd see how this particular bar made one,
or whether, to be friendly, she was having one because I was.
I got it from the bar as quickly as I could, feeling strangely
responsible for her there. I didn't want anyone to bother her.

"What were you thinking about?" she said. "You were
very far away."

I explained about Christopher Isherwood. She knew
that part of Santa Monica where the writer lived. She became most interested in something Isherwood had told me. It
had been mystical and, to me, a little hard to grasp, but she
seemed to follow immediately, as if it was close to one of her

own ideas. I got out my notebook to read Isherwood's exact words to her: "I didn't decide to live here. It just happened, as with all the places I've lived. One grows older and changes, but one also changes with the places a little. If one didn't grow old and die, and if one could just be kept in a state of being at the physical age of about thirty-five or forty, I think one would probably go back and forth over a pattern of selves. But as we don't have the experience, it's impossible to tell."

She liked that—"a pattern of selves." She thought many people made the mistake of thinking of themselves as one consistent self during their entire lives. How much more tolerant they would be of other people if they understood their own fragmentary, changing natures! "I certainly change with places and people. I'm different in New York than I am in Hollywood. I'm different here in this bar than at the studio. But the same happens with people. I'm different with Lee than with my secretary, and I'm different again with you. I always see that in interviews. The questions demand certain answers and make you seem a certain kind of person. The questions often tell more about the interviewer than the answers do about me."

"You seduce interviewers." I grinned to show I wasn't attacking her. "You don't want them to get at the real you, but to fall in love with you and write love stories."

"You think so?"

"Oh, yes." Still grinning, unsure of her.

"Well, it didn't work with you. I had to come over to talk with you."

"Professional pride."

"Okay, I like it better. I don't respect people who like you because you're famous. If I was unknown, they wouldn't be interested."

"Maybe in a different way. Isherwood also said: 'What is very important is not to repudiate anything you have ever been, but to realize you will change and to accept it.'"

"Just repudiate other people and start again."

"People who don't like you say you discard people too easily."

That was a hard remark to make on such a short acquaintance, and she frowned at the thought that there were people who didn't like her. "I've never dropped anyone I believed in. My trouble is, I trust people too much. I believe in them too much and I go on believing in them when the signs are already there. You get a lot of disappointments." She sat back, gloomy with memories. I mentioned hurriedly that Charles Laughton had a house next door to Isherwood's, knowing that she and Laughton had appeared together in the movie *O. Henry's Full House*. Her mood changed immediately and her whole face brightened.

She leaned forward confidingly, full of fun. "He played a gentlemen bum and I was a lady streetwalker." She giggled. "I was overawed at first, but he was very nice to me. He accepted me as an equal. I enjoyed working with him. He was like a character out of Charles Dickens." She looked at me with a strange expression, almost like a student seeking approval, and her voice became more like the little-girl tone she used in some of her movies—the defenseless blonde, the overawed young actress. She was playing a scene, teasing me. "At first I felt like I was acting with a king or somebody great—like a god!"

"That's the impression I get of Lee Strasberg," I said, testing her.

"Oh, Lee's not like that—not when you know him and he's interested in your work. But I guess he overawed me, too, at the beginning."

"He's not like a Dickens character?"

"No, Lee's made himself. He's not like anybody."

I recalled that when I'd interviewed Laughton a couple of years before, he'd told me: "People have seen every aspect of me by now and they know what to expect—old Laughton cooked up."

She smiled, showing teeth that were not as film-star white as I expected. "He didn't really believe that, but I can understand him feeling that way. I sometimes feel like that and I'm much younger than he is. I sometimes feel as if I'm too exposed. I've given myself away, the whole of me, every part, and there's nothing left that's private, just me alone. If you feel low, you might worry that there's nothing new to give. But that's not true—not ever. You discover things inside yourself you never knew were there. You always go on developing. A teacher like Lee helps you to uncover all the secret sides of yourself." She ended rather breathless, watching me eagerly for my response, as if it really mattered to her.

"It doesn't make you too self-conscious? You remember the story of the centipede who wondered how he did it—and fell over his own feet."

She laughed merrily. "Lee would hate that story. You've got to understand what you're doing. You've got to know yourself."

She was very defensive about Strasberg. It was better to

stay off the subject, at least for now. I went back to Laughton because he seemed to interest her. I recalled that his wife Elsa Lanchester, a rather plain woman but a good character actress, had come in while we were talking, and Laughton, like a smoldering volcano, had said to me in a gruff, challenging voice: "Don't you think my wife's pretty?"

Marilyn liked that. She laughed so loudly that some people at the bar peered back at us. "He was being a loyal husband. They were married a long time, weren't they?"

"Twenty or thirty years, I think."

"I wish I could achieve a settled relationship like that," she said wistfully. "Someone always to come home to, someone always interested in what you're doing—and helping you over the tough spots, helping each other. I've come to love that line, 'until death do us part.' It always seems to go well for a time, and then something happens. Maybe it's me."

She meant it to sound joking, but she looked so sad about it, as though she'd touched a sore spot, that I hurried on with a Laughton postscript. It was four o'clock in the afternoon when I met him, but he was still in his bathrobe, his hair awry, sleep still in his eyes. When I described him that way in the article I wrote about him, he phoned me, very indignant. Readers would think actors were lazy, he said. He'd been up "for hours."

Marilyn chuckled, no longer sad. "He was only being defensive. I understand him. People have such strange ideas about actors. They seldom respect you. I recently met a suburban couple and the woman acted as if I was there to seduce her husband. She insisted on sitting between us. I wasn't respectable in her eyes."

"But don't you try to seduce every man you meet?" I was trying to keep her in a joking mood. "Don't you like to feel your power over them?" I said it humorously, but I meant it.

"Sometimes I hate the effect I have on people. I get tired of stupid attention, of working people up. It's not really a human thing." As if fearing that that sounded too self-pitying, she touched my notebook, still open at my notes of the Isherwood interview. "I hope our little drink isn't going in that notebook."

"Oh, no." I drew back, a little offended. Surely she could trust me more than that.

She touched my hand impulsively. "I was only joking. If I didn't trust you, I wouldn't be here. Don't be hurt so easily. I thought you reporters were supposed to be hard-boiled, like us Hollywood actresses. You're the first shy reporter I've ever met. You're like me—an old softie. I liked the way you went to see Mrs. Chekhov, but you didn't immediately run off and write about it. Put me in the notebook if you like, but don't write about it now. Do it when I retire." She said it with a mocking smile—mocking herself?

"I'll retire before you—or be dead."

"Oh, no, you look too healthy." She smiled happily. She was in a smiling mood, as if trying to raise her own spirits, as well as mine. But everything she said seemed to turn strangely serious. She gave me the impression of a child whistling (or laughing) in the dark. The more she tried to cheer herself up, the more she seemed aware of the dark around her, threatening her. "What have you been doing since I saw you in Hollywood?"

I could have answered the question with some flip

remark, but the only real compliment I ever paid her to her face was always to reply seriously to anything she said. I sense that she thought too many people didn't take her seriously. She also seemed to pay me (and everyone else) the same compliment. When she was with you, she gave you her whole attention.

I tried to explain to her what happened in New Orleans.

"Money," she said. "That's what it's all about. It's easy to understand the slave system when you've been through the star system." She asked me about Christine. "I once had an affair with a young Negro man," she said seriously. "He would never meet me in public—and I don't think I wanted to. I think we were both too scared. I used to sort of sidle into his room when nobody was looking. We liked each other. He understood me very well. But it couldn't last in those conditions. It was like trying to love someone in jail. It only lasts while you're inside. And in the end, you want to get out. You do. You want your freedom. I don't even know what happened to him. I hoped he'd see one of my movies and write to me, but maybe he just wanted to forget."

I told her about Christine's and James Baldwin's admiration of her. "Negroes seem able to identify with you; yet, as a blonde star, you're a white symbol."

She was impatient with that. "I don't want to be a symbol of anything. Negros can sometimes see through appearances better than whites. Blondes don't even appeal to some of them. I'm not a sex symbol, but busty Miss Anne," and she laughed merrily, her bust rising beneath her blouse. "Gee," she said, "we *are* talking seriously. I thought this was to be a drunken party."

"Let's get drunk then." I brought her another drink from the bar.

"I read your article about me," she said. "Who's Mrs. Patrick Campbell?"

I had described her in the article as a cross between a theatrical grandame like Mrs. Campbell and a child star like Shirley Temple.

She beamed when I told her, but she added that she took a dim view of being even remotely compared to "Lolita Temple."

"Sorry. Now that I know you better, I wouldn't compare you to anyone."

"All is forgiven. Do you enjoy interviewing?"

"Only if I learn what the person is really like."

"Do you ever do that? I mean, aren't most interviews too short? And don't people play roles?"

"Sometimes one catches a glimpse of the truth."

"I must be careful," she said.

"You're safe. We've agreed I won't write anything."

"And you keep your agreements?"

"A reporter has to."

"Okay," she said, as if she were satisfied. "What are you reading at present?"

It was my turn to laugh. It reminded me of an English joke. When there was an uneasy silence between strangers, one always asked: "Have you read any good books recently?" I explained it to her.

"But I'm serious."

"I recently read Norman Mailer's *The Deer Park*. It might interest you. It's about Hollywood. I'll get you a copy."

"Do you ever feel some books are beyond you? I mean, your mind can't handle them?"

"Yes, certain philosophical works in translation. It's almost like a foreign language though the words are English."

"It makes me feel so dumb sometimes."

"I wouldn't worry about it if I were you. You have sharper instincts than many intellectuals. You don't want to blunt your instincts just for the sake of secondhand knowledge. I'd rather be beautiful than wise."

She frowned, and I felt as if I'd made a bad error. "That sounds like Sir Olivier telling me to be sexy. I'd rather be wise. I wish I'd had a longer formal education. Sometimes when Arthur and his friends were talking, I couldn't follow. I don't know much about politics. I'm just past the goodies and baddies stage. The politicians get away with murder because most Americans don't know any more about it than I do. Less even. Arthur was always very good at explaining, but I felt at my age I should have known. It's my country and I should know what they're doing with it." She sat up. "What time is it?"

I stood up and looked at the bar clock. It was after six.

"I must go. I'm going out to dinner with some friends. Want to come?"

"I've got a dinner date."

"I hope it's not with a girl," she said severely. "You must be loyal to Christine. Many American men are very disloyal and yet they expect their women to be loyal to them."

"I've just had a drink with the world's sex symbol. Christine might not think that was loyal."

"We're just friends," she said as if she were speaking to reporters. She laughed and got up. "I must fly. I'll be very late. But people expect that. Some friends give me the time an hour early so I'll arrive on time. You don't need to come out with me."

"I'll see you to a cab."

I hoped she wouldn't be recognized going out. I didn't feel like acting as her bodyguard. But she was very cool. It was a familiar situation for her and she could turn the magnet on or off. Now it was off. One's eyes automatically followed her rear, but there was no wiggle of waggle in her walk. Several men stared, but no one called out after her.

"Have you time for me to find a bookstore and get you *The Deer Park*?"

"If you want to," she said obligingly.

We walked a few blocks along Eighth Avenue. People were still going home, rushing toward the subway or the Port Authority Bus Terminal, and she blended in easily with the crowd, without fuss or seeking attention. Most people were in such a hurry that they didn't even glance at us. A middle-aged wino with a black, ravaged face stopped us for a quarter. She gave him one and he thanked her very courteously. I hurried her on.

"I should have given him a dollar," she said, looking back with concern. "I wasn't thinking."

"He was pleased anyway."

But she wasn't satisfied until she went back and gave the man a dollar. He couldn't have been more surprised if a gold brick had fallen out of the sky. She smiled shyly at him, embarrassed.

Such actions are not missed on Eighth Avenue. We hadn't gone far before a flower-seller waylaid us, an old woman with a solid, cheery Irish face. I bought Marilyn a red rose and she stuck it in her head scarf so that the rose came over the right side of her head.

"That looks pretty," the old woman said, peering at Marilyn. "Don't I know your face darlin'?" Oh, I thought, here it comes. I watched recognition slowly dawn. "Aren't you Marilyn Monroe?"

Marilyn nodded, smiling.

"How're you doin', darlin'?" the woman asked, squeezing her hand.

"Pretty well," Marilyn said, giving the old woman her whole attention. "How're you doin', yourself?"

"Can't complain, Marilyn dear. Sorry you and your old man split up. You have as bad luck with men as I do. Better luck next time. Keep smilin' darlin'."

Marilyn smiled. "Good luck, flower lady."

But it wasn't so easy to escape. The old woman wanted an autograph, but she had no paper. I tore a page out of my notebook. Marilyn asked her her name and wrote her a good luck message and signed it. The old woman beamed. "That's luvly, Marilyn."

We walked quickly away as the old woman looked around for someone to tell. News that Marilyn Monroe was there would soon be all over Eighth Avenue.

We found a paperback bookstore and I bought her *The Deer Park*.

"I'll read it," she said, "and I'll tell you what I think of it."

I stopped a cab for her. The driver had an alert, knowing face, and I bet he would recognize her before he got her home. Her disguise wasn't all that good.

She said through the open window: "Let's do this again. It was fun. I enjoyed it."

"I did, too," I said. "Are you being polite or serious?"

"Serious."

"When then?"

"Day after tomorrow." She added apologetically, "I've got business all day tomorrow."

We made a date for the same bar. She said she liked it.

I waved her off and then went in a snack bar to make some notes of our conversation. In those days of constant heavyweight interviewing, I had a good, practiced memory for conversations, so I remembered what Marilyn had said even if I didn't perhaps always remember her exact words. I still wondered if she was just being friendly or whether she had a purpose behind it all. But what purpose could she have? If I wasn't writing anything, I was of no use to her career. Suspicion still lingered like poison.

[* * *]

She arrived in a different mood, coming into the bar this time very tentatively and nervously, nearly an hour late. She stood uneasily near the bar, looking around, and I rushed to meet her. She was dressed in the same sloppy way. Because of her nervousness, she seemed even less like the famous star.

"I'm late," she said as if I might scold her.

I got her a drink. A gin and tonic, I think. Her manner seemed rather distant when I joined her at the table and I wondered if she'd had a lot to drink already. Maybe it was pills.

"I nearly didn't come," she said.

"I'm glad you did."

"I felt like staying inside—away from people."

"You got the blues?"

"Sort of." She took a quick drink. "I saw Monty Clift. That man is beautiful, but he's killing himself slowly." She laughed nervously. "Or not so slowly."

"I heard he'd been seen in the bathhouses."

"What does he need that for? He's sort of running away from himself." She grinned. "I know the feeling." She burrowed in her bag and brought out the copy of *The Deer Park* I'd given her and pushed it across the table. "He's too impressed by power, in my opinion."

"I thought he understood it."

"You can't fool me about that," she said. "I've felt that way myself—scared of being a loser." And to back it up, she told me again the story about Betty Grable she'd told me in Reno. "They won't ever humiliate me that way. I'm going into the theater or character acting—or I'm just *going*. I'll never wait for them to say 'so long.' I've had fame, but maybe I can learn to live without it. What do you think?"

"I'm sure you could. It might even have its advantages. Personal relationships must be easier."

"You don't attract so many heels. Sometimes I've got such lousy taste in men. There was a whole period when I felt flattered if a man took interest in me—any man! I believed too easily in people, and then I went on believing in them even after they disappointed me over and over again. I must have been very stupid in those days. I guess I'm capable of doing it again with some guy, only he'd have to be someone more outstanding than a heel. Not that I didn't pay for it all   all I've ever done. There were times when I'd be with one of my husbands and I'd run into one of those Hollywood heels at a party and they'd paw me cheaply in front of everybody as if they were saying, *Oh, we had her.* I guess it's the classic situation of an ex-whore, though I was never a whore in that sense. I was never kept; I always kept myself. But there was a period when I responded too much to flattery and slept around too much, thinking it would help my career, though I always liked the guy at the time. They were always so full of self-confidence and I had none at all and they made me feel better. But you don't get self-confidence that way. You have to get it by earning respect. I've never given up on anyone who I thought respected me." Her eyes were wide and her gaze direct, as if she were appealing to be believed.

"I'm sure you've been respected far more than you realize."

"Do you really think so?"

"People respect you because they feel you've survived hard times and endured, and although you've become famous, you haven't become phony."

"Thank you," she said. "I've certainly tried." She sat back and relaxed a little. "You must excuse me if I'm not good company. I've been having trouble sleeping. It makes me grumpy. I used to have a bad temper, but I try to control it nowadays. Poor Arthur, he saw some of it. Flashes of lightning and thunder! That's why I try and be sweet, but sometimes it's not possible."

I told her about my meeting with Paula Strasberg. "She and Lee Strasberg really believe you're going to be a great stage actress."

"Oh, I hope. I'm working very hard to be good enough to have the confidence. Their belief in me helps me to keep going, especially when I'm not sleeping and haven't much energy. They work so hard with me on the essentials—like a pianist and his scales. Projection, movement, breath control—all those things. And I'm doing short scenes like I did with Mr. Chekhov. I read once the role of Blanche du Bois in Tennessee Williams's *A Streetcar Named Desire*. I'd like to play that on Broadway when I'm older. I like the last line so much. She says—I forget the exact words—something about she's always had to depend on strangers for kindness. I know what she meant. Friends and relatives can let you down. You can depend on them too much. But don't depend *too* much on strangers, honey. Some strangers gave me hard time when I was a kid."

"I read once that you were raped as a child."

"Don't let's talk about that. I'm tired of talking about that. I'm sorry I ever mentioned it to anyone." She absentmindedly wiped the table with a paper napkin and then grinned at herself. "The housewife. I enjoy housework. Takes my mind off things. But thinking of what Blanche said, do you know who I've always depended on? Not strangers, not friends. The telephone! That's my best friend. I seldom write letters, but I love calling friends, especially late at night when I can't sleep. I have this dream we all get up and go out to a drugstore."

"Schwab's?"

"No, that scene sort of depresses me." She played with her drink, thinking. "I was remembering Monty Clift. People who aren't fit to open the door for him sneer at his homosexuality. What do they know about it? Labels—people love

putting labels on each other. Then they feel safe. People tried
to make me into a lesbian. I laughed. No sex is wrong if
there's love in it. But too often people act like it's gymnasium
work, mechanical. They'd be as satisfied with a machine from
a drugstore as with another human being. I sometimes felt
they were trying to make me into a machine." She smiled
with what looked like embarrassment and took a sip of her
drink. But she didn't let go of the subject. It was as if there
was something bugging her. She might have been talking to
herself as she went on.

"I sometimes felt I was hooked on sex, the way an alcoholic is on liquor or a junkie on dope. My body turned all
these people on, like turning on an electric light, and there
was so rarely anything human in it. Marilyn Monroe became
a burden, a—what do you call it?—an albatross. People expected so much of me, I sometimes hated them. It was too
much of a strain. I still feel that way. Marilyn Monroe has
to look a certain way—be *beautiful*—and act a certain way,
be talented. I wondered if I could live up to their expecta-
tions. There were times on *The Misfits*, in those emotional
scenes, when I had a feeling I'd fail however hard I'd try, and
I didn't want to go to the set in the morning. I was sorry then
I wasn't a waitress or a cleaning lady and free of people's great
demands. Sometimes it would be a big relief to be no longer
famous. But we actors and actresses are such worriers, such—
what is your word?—Narcissus types. I sit in front of the
mirror for hours looking for signs of age. Yet I like old people;
they have great qualities younger peoples don't have. I want
to grow old without face-lifts. They take the life out of a face,
the character. I want to have the courage to be loyal to the

face I've made. Sometimes I think it would be easier to avoid old age, to die young, but then you'd never complete your life, would you? You'd never wholly know yourself."

"Lots of people don't want to know themselves."

"I don't think I'm like that," she said seriously. "But sometimes I get scared of finding out. For a long time I was scared I'd find out that I was like my mother and end up in the crazy house. I wonder when I break down if I'm not tough enough—like her. But I'm hoping to get stronger." Her spirits seemed to rise. "I ask myself, 'What am I afraid of?' I know I have talent. I know I can act. Well, get on with it, Marilyn. I feel I still try to ingratiate myself with people, try to tell them what they want to hear. That's fear, too. We should all start to live before we get too old. Fear is stupid. So are regrets. You know, for years I had this big regret that I hadn't gotten a high school diploma. What does it matter now? All those high school diploma-holders would love to be movie stars. You've got to keep your sense of proportion. I guess that diploma kinda represents for me a home, a security I never really had. I was never used to being happy. For years I thought having a father and being married meant happiness. I've never had a father—you can't *buy* them!—but I've been married three times and haven't found permanent happiness yet. You've got to get the most out of the moment. Let's make some mischief." She laughed and looked around the bar. Suddenly she way gay, as though she'd come out on the other side of some confused, unhappy mood.

"Would you like to dance on the bar?" I asked, trying to match her new mood and feeling the obviousness of my attempt. But she wasn't the kind of person who wanted you to succeed every time; she gave you marks for trying.

"We'd only be thrown out," she said gleefully. She made me feel like I had made a good joke. "This is a men's bar. Women have to lie low."

Not Marilyn Monroe, I thought. She could take it over and have all the tough guys at the bar eating out of her hand. But she looked shy then, as if asserting herself was the last thing she had in mind. Fear of rejection seemed to be more in her thoughts.

"What would Mae West do?" she said, chuckling.

"Probably wrestle the bartender."

"I learned a few tricks from her—that impression of laughing at, or mocking, her own sexuality."

"You are a *beautiful* Mae West!"

"She's a handsome woman." In an accurate Mae West voice she said: "Come up and see me sometime." She pushed her glass away. "You know what I'd like? A cup of coffee."

"There's a snack bar next door." She began to get up. "No, wait here. I'll bring you one." She'd be much more visible in a well-lit snack bar, and I wanted her to myself a little longer.

She was dabbing at her nose when I returned with a container of coffee.

"Does my nose look kinda shiny?"

"No, it looks fine."

"You're a great help." She gulped some coffee. "I hope the bartender won't object to me drinking coffee from outside."

"He's too busy to notice. But if he comes over, just flash him a smile."

"You think that would work?" She gave a glassy mechanical smile.

"Put a little more love into it."

She laughed. She was in a strange mood, all right.

"You know, I've been thinking of writing my will. Can't tell you why, but it's been on my mind. It's made me feel sort of gloomy. I always thought you did that when you were old or sick, but people tell me everyone oughta make a will if you've got something to leave. Saves a lot of trouble. I haven't got any fortune now, but maybe I'll make something out of *The Misfits*. Anyways it's on my mind. Without a will, everything'd go to my mother, I guess, and what would she do with it?"

"Have you seen the complete film of *The Misfits*?"

"I'm still too close to it. Some people say it's pretty good. I wonder what the critics will say." She sounded anxious.

"They'll praise your performance."

"Oh, I hope. I wish Clark were still alive to see it. I felt guilty when he died, in case I'd put too much strain on him while we were making the movie. But that was stupid. He had a bad heart. No one can give you that. But he was such a strong, upright man—a real gentleman—that it was a great shock. Like your father dying. I wept all night. I'd have gone to his funeral, but I was afraid of breaking down. I loved that man. I wish we could have met when we were both young and about the same age, but I guess it probably wouldn't have worked out. When you're both famous, it's a double problem—even when you're famous in different ways, like Arthur and I were."

Her eyes widened, as though she couldn't quite believe what she was thinking. "Fame causes such envy. People hate you sometimes just because you're famous. They're phony to your face. See you around—like never. I like to be accepted for my own sake, but a lot of people don't care who you *are*. All they're interested in is your fame—while you've got it. I like to escape it, like we're doing now. When I was a kid, the world often seemed a pretty grim place. I loved to escape through games and make-believe. You can do that even better as an actress, but sometimes it seems you escape altogether and people never let you come back. You're trapped in your fame. Maybe I'll never get out of it now until it's over. Fame has gone and I'm old. What should I do then? I don't think it'll throw me. I have ideas. I'll be interested in *everything*. Character acting, poetry reading, yoga, travel—everything. That's the way to stay alive. It is," she said, laughing self-consciously.

She finished her coffee. Silence.

"Balzac was the world's greatest coffee-drinker," I said to break the silence.

"The French writer?" Again that uncertain look.

"He wrote from late night until the next day on thick black coffee, to keep himself awake."

"Didn't he ever sleep?"

"If you read his biography, it's hard to see how he had the time. He died when he was fifty, worn out."

"I wonder how I'll feel when I'm fifty. Half a century!"

"You'll probably feel completely at peace with yourself."

"I hope so. When's your birthday?"

"January 8."

"What's your sign?"

"Capricorn."

"The goat!"

"What's yours?"

"Gemini."

"What kind of people are Geminis?"

"Jekyll and Hyde. Two in one."

"And that's you?"

"More than two. I'm so many people. They shock me sometimes. I wish I was just *me*! I used to think maybe I was going crazy, until I discovered some people I admired were like that, too. Arthur's about seven hundred different people." She laughed, looking a little embarrassed. Suddenly she was off in another direction. She was a restless conversationalist. "Do people ever get over being shy? I think it's with you for life—like the color of your eyes."

"Maybe inside. You can learn to handle it outside, hide it. You've learned to do it, right?"

"Not always. Sometimes I *freeze*." She looked very serious. "I could have got so much more done if I had more self-confidence."

I told her what Tennessee Williams had told me, that he had no self-confidence about his work. Her remark about escaping from the world also reminded me of what he had said about escaping through his writing. "You two sound alike."

"Maybe too much alike—like me and Monty Clift. You don't look for someone like yourself. You look for someone different with different qualities. Nobody could be more unlike the men I've been friendly with—Arthur and Joe and Frank and . . . and, and, and . . . so many, yet here I am alone. I don't like being alone. Nobody does. It puts too many pressures on you. But sometimes it keeps you out of trouble."

"It can also get you *into* trouble."

"How?"

"You want company, so you choose any company, which sometimes means bad company."

"Yes, that's true. I've done that. I must be careful now not to do it again. I've been with some stinkers."

"Everybody has." My remark sounded feeble. But she made me want to say something to help, and I didn't know what.

"Even the stinkers go with stinkers." That amused her, and she sat back and laughed. Wanting the mood to change, she was trying to force herself to feel gay.

I told her the old story about Harold Ross, the founder-editor of *The New Yorker* magazine, when someone complained that the women in James Thurber's drawings had no sex appeal. "They do for Thurber's men," he is supposed to have replied.

"You mean stinkers aren't stinkers to stinkers," she said very seriously, as though trying to work out a complicated mathematical equation.

"I guess they're not."

"It all depends on where you're coming from."

"What you're standing on."

"What you are," she said.

A friend of hers had told me: "Conversations with Marilyn are apt to get suddenly serious and go anywhere." I could see what she meant. I felt bad about not being able to keep her in a gay mood when she was trying so hard to raise her spirits, but maybe it wasn't my fault.

She watched a grey cat walk lazily across the top of the bar. "If that was a rat, they'd all run for cover—"

"Or try to kill it. A rat's dangerous."

"Someone told me they're only dangerous if you attack them first."

"Don't believe it."

"A cat can be dangerous, too."

"Not many. They're exceptions. Cats leave you alone."

"Depends where they are." She suddenly laughed. "I'm going out on a limb. Have you ever noticed how you can talk yourself into saying impossible things?"

"I used to report what politicians said. They're always saying impossible things."

"John Kennedy talks sense," she said firmly.

"Not all the time."

"Oh, he does."

"Did you see where he's made his brother, Bobby, attorney general?"

She looked surprised. Her knowledge of current events seemed to be spotty. "Keeping it in the family, huh? How many Kennedys are there? Maybe he'll give them all jobs and it'll be a Kennedy government." She laughed. "They say their father made them all millionaires."

"You sound respectful."

"I admire their zest, the impression they give of enjoying life. It's so rare in our public life. Public figures generally seem like stuffed shirts or tombstones—monuments. If you don't enjoy life, you're wasting your time here, but so many of us make that mistake."

"I think that's one reason you're so popular with movie-goers: you seem to be enjoying yourself."

That pleased her. "You think so?"

"They also identify with you as Cinderella."

"Cinderella? That's as bad as Lolita Temple."

"I mean the beautiful poor girl who has overcome."

"I haven't overcome. I wish I had!"

"To moviegoers, you have. You're a star!"

"Whatever that means, however much it's worth." She looked wistful for a moment and then smiled, gay again. "But don't knock it. It can set you free. Where would I be without it? On a calendar—nude." She grinned. "How shocked some of the studio people were at the time, and now it seems like nothing. I enjoyed doing it. I'm on close terms with my body because I look after it. I don't mistreat it. But sometimes I feel infatuated by it. I'm too much into it then. When the photographers come, it's like looking in a mirror. They think they arrange me to suit themselves, but I use them to put over myself. It's necessary in the movie business, but I often hate it. I never show it, though. It could ruin me. I need their goodwill. I'm not stupid. Even Arthur used to go over the pictures, helping me spot the bad ones. Of course, the bad ones were those that didn't make me seem beautiful." She giggled at that.

"I felt occasionally that I was killing the truth when I killed the ones that were bad for my public image. Here is Marilyn Monroe with egg on her face. I used to feel as tied to the beauty business as an addict to his drugs. It's a relief to get in sloppy clothes and not worry about the impression you're making—about any of it. But it's part of my career—my life!—and I accept it. When my looks start to go, so will most of the fans. *So long, it's been nice knowing you.* But I won't care. I'll be ready. There's other kinds of beauty, other ways of impressing people and getting over. I hope to do it by sheer acting. I *do*," she added, as if I were going to challenge it—or laugh. "You can go on forever in the theater. The distance, the footlights, the makeup—it all helps create whatever illusion you wish. Who was that great actress you compared me to?"

"Shirley Temple?"

She gave me a mock snarl.

"Mrs. Patrick Campbell."

"Mrs. Marilyn Monroe. How does that sound?" She was working herself up into a merry mood again. It seemed like a constant struggle that day not to lapse into sadness. She also seemed obsessed with the idea of the theater as her salvation. It was something she was clutching at, but I wondered how substantial it would be if she had nothing else left. I kept seeing her arriving an hour late, or in the ninetieth performance, forgetting her lines in a crucial scene, and then her agonized look of breakdown. All actors and actresses, I thought, when they stare so much at themselves, must stare also at all their bad dreams. They have to have great strength to live so closely with such dreams. Marilyn Monroe was undoubtedly a tough professional in many ways, but she also seemed frail and vulnerable. How much of this side of her was an act for sympathy, a part of the seduction scene?

I still didn't know the answer, but as if to remind me of it, she leaned over and stroked the bar cat which had finished inspecting the regulars at the bar and had come down to sniff us. "I wonder if he's an alcoholic," she said. "He's very skinny. They probably feed him liquor instead of food." The cat purred under her careful stroking. "I think he's a bit high now." She mumbled something to the cat that sounded like "mumble-bumble-dee." The cat didn't seem very interested. "I asked him in cat language what his favorite drink was."

"What did he say?"

"Milk—but he doesn't get much. It's harder to get here than Scotch whiskey!"

"Poor cat."

"He's not *poor*. He's tough. You shouldn't pity animals. It's superior. We're all poor."

"I'm sorry. I meant to be sympathetic."

"Well"—she smiled—"We can't love everyone, I guess. I've done my share of trying." Suddenly she looked sad again. The gay mood was over. She stopped stroking the cat. "Time to go," she said. "I'm hours late already." I felt she was just getting away to be by herself so she wouldn't have to make so much of an effort. For some reason I didn't know, it was a bad day for her.

THE LAST INTERVIEW: "A LAST LONG TALK WITH A LONELY GIRL"

CONVERSATION WITH RICHARD MERYMAN
LIFE
AUGUST 17, 1962

Only a few weeks before her death Marilyn Monroe talked at length to
LIFE *Associate Editor Richard Meryman about the effects of fame on her
life. Her story was published in the August 3 issue. Here he recalls what
Marilyn was like as she talked to him.*

If Marilyn Monroe was glad to see you, her "hello" will sound
in your mind all of your life—the breathless warmth of the
emphasis on the "lo," her well-deep eyes turned up toward
you and her face radiantly crinkled in a wonderfully girlish
smile.

I first experienced this when, after two get-acquainted
meetings in New York, I came in the late afternoon several
weeks ago to her Brentwood, California home to begin a series
of conversations on fame. Expecting one of the famous waits
for Marilyn, I sat on the soft wall-to-wall carpet of the living
room and began struggling to set up my tape recorder. Suddenly, I became aware of a pair of brilliant yellow slacks upright
beside me. In the slacks was Marilyn, silently watching me
with a solicitous grin, very straight and slender with delicately
narrow shoulders. She seemed shorter than I remembered and

she looked spectacular in a loose-fitting blouse. I stood up and we greeted and she said, "Do you want my tape recorder? I bought one to play the poems of a friend of mine."

Before starting what was to be no less than a six-hour talk, she wanted to show me her house which she had personally searched out and bought. Describing it earlier she exclaimed, ". . . and it has *walls.*" She had refused *LIFE* any pictures of it, saying, "I don't want *everybody* to see exactly where I live, what my sofa or my fireplace looks like. Do you know the book *Everyman*? Well, I want to stay just in the fantasy of Everyman."

It was a small, three-bedroom house built in Mexican style, the first home entirely her own she had ever had. She exulted in it. On a special trip to Mexico she had carefully searched in roadside stands and shops and even factories to find just the right things to put in it. The large items had not arrived—nor was she ever to see them installed. As she led me through the rooms, bare and makeshift as though someone lived there only temporarily, she described with loving excitement each couch and table and dresser, where it would go and what was special about it. The few small Mexican things—a tin candelabra, folding stools ingeniously carved from single pieces of wood, a leather-covered coffee table, tiles on the kitchen walls—revealed her impetuous, charming taste. Separate from the house, attached to her two-car garage, was a large room being converted to an apartment which would be, she explained, "a place for any friends of mine who are in some kind of trouble, you know, and maybe they'll want to live here where they won't be bothered till things are okay for them."

Back in the house I remarked on the profusion of flowers outside. Her face grew bright and she said, "I don't know why but I've always been able to make anything grow." She went on: "When I was married to Mr. Miller, we celebrated Hanukkah and I felt, well, we should also have a Christmas tree. But I couldn't stand the idea of going out and chopping off a Christmas tree."

In the living room, seated on a nondescript chair and sofa, we went on talking—after Marilyn poured herself a glass of champagne. At each question she paused thoughtfully. "I'm trying to find the nail-head, not just strike the blow," she said. Then a deep breath and out her thoughts would tumble, breathless words falling over breathless words. Once she said, "One way basically to handle fame is with honesty and I mean it and the other way to handle it when something happens—as things have happened recently, and I've had other things happen to me, suddenly, my goodness, the things they try to do to you, it's hard to take—I handle with silence."

Her inflections came as surprising twists and every emotion was in full bravura, acted out with exuberant gestures. Across her face flashed anger, wistfullness, bravado, tenderness, ruefulness, high humor and deep sadness. And each idea usually ended in a startling turn of thought, with her laugh rising to a delightful squeak. "I think I have always had a little humor," said Marilyn. "I guess sometimes people just sort of questioned, 'does she know what she's saying,' and sometimes you do all of a sudden think about something else and you didn't mean to say it exactly. I'm pointing at me. I don't digest things with my mind. If I did, the whole thing wouldn't work. Then I'd just be kind of an intellectual and that I'm not interested in."

At this point I began to see that Marilyn did nothing by halves. Of her millions of fans she said, "The least I can is give them the best they can get from me. What's the good of drawing in the next breath if all you do is let it out and draw in another?" I could also see how important it was to her to feel that the person she talked to "understood."

Understanding apparently meant being very sympathetic, taking her side in everything, recognizing the nuances of her meanings and valuing all that she valued, especially small things. When I showed genuine enthusiasm for her house, she said, "Good, anybody who likes my house, I'm sure I'll get along with."

But I had the constant, uneasy feeling that my status with her was precarious, that if I grew the least bit careless, she might suddenly decide that I, like many others she felt had let her down, did not understand. Once I slangily asked her how she "cranked up" to do a scene. I was instantly confronted by queenly outrage: "I don't crank anything. I'm not a Model T. I think that's kind of disrespectful to refer to it that way."

But I could not feel impatient with her impatience. It was all so understandable as she talked about the people who wrote columns and stories about her: "They go around and ask mostly your enemies. Friends always say, 'Let's check and see if this is all right with her.'" And then she added wistfully: "You know, most people really don't know me." There was grief in her eyes when she described how she had once found her stepson Bobby Miller hiding a magazine containing a lurid article about her, and how Joe DiMaggio Jr. used to be taunted at school because of her.

"You know, ha, ha, your stepmother is Marilyn Monroe, ha, ha, ha. All that kind of stuff." And there was yearning in her voice as she returned over and over again to "kids, and older people and workingmen" as a source of warmth in her life, as the unthreatening people who treated her naturally, whom she could meet spontaneously. I felt a rush of protectiveness for her; a wish—perhaps the sort that was the root of the public's tenderness for Marilyn—to keep her from anything ugly and hurtful.

Before I left late that night, she asked to be sent a transcript of the interview. "I often wake up in the night," she explained, "and I like to have something to think about."

When I arrived the next afternoon for a second session she immediately asked to postpone our talk. She was tired out, she said, from negotiations with 20th Century-Fox over resumption of *Something's Got to Give*. But she hospitably offered me a drink and we chatted. She was obviously upset. But there was no hint of morose despair. She was electric with indignation and began talking angrily about how studios treat their stars. Then she paused, said she needed something to help overcome her tiredness and got a glass of champagne. I asked if she had ever wished that she were tougher. She answered, "Yes—but I don't think it would be very feminine to be tough. Guess I'll settle for the way I am."

We were interrupted when her doctor arrived. Marilyn bounded out to the kitchen, returned with a little ampule, and holding it up to me said, "No kidding, they're making me take liver shots. Here, I'll prove it to you." By then she was willing to talk on, and it was nearly midnight when Marilyn jumped up and announced she was going to throw a steak on the grill. She came back to say there was no steak and no food at all. Before I left one of the last things she said was, "With fame, you know, you can read about yourself, somebody else's ideas about you, but what's important is how you feel about yourself—for survival and living day to day with what comes up."

Over the weekend Marilyn was scheduled to pose for pictures so I suggested we eat breakfast before her noon appointment. She agreed and I arrived on Saturday at ten. I rang the doorbell repeatedly. No answer. But through the window I could see a man sitting in her little glassed-in porch, reading a magazine with the bored patience of somebody who had been there a long time. I waited and rang for about ten minutes, then went away for an hour. At eleven my ring was answered by Marilyn's housekeeper, Mrs. Murray, who took me to wait in a guest room just off a tiny hall from Marilyn's bedroom. At noon Mrs. Murray took a tray of breakfast in to her. Shortly afterward Marilyn came out and said hello.

I then became a witness to the fabled process of Marilyn preparing for an appointment—and being four hours late for it. The patient gentleman was her hairdresser, Mr. Kenneth. While he worked on her and she sat under the dryer I could hear uproarious laughter. Then, in her curlers, she made little barefooted errands about the house and in and out of her room, phone calls, visits to me to ask if I was comfortable, all busy bustling, getting nothing done. There was none of the fearful moping and preening in front of mirrors I had heard so much about. She was entirely cheerful and utterly disorganized. I could not help feeling that what some people blamed on stage fright might partly be her endless debt to time. The necessary mechanics of daily living were beyond her grasp; she always started out behind and never caught up.

Finally she was almost ready and she came trippingly into the room where I sat. She wore high heels, orange slacks, a brassiere, and held an orange blouse carelessly across her bosom. "Do I look like a pumpkin in this outfit?" she asked. She looked wonderful. "You'll set the fashion industry ahead ten years." I said. She was very pleased and answered, "You think so? Good!"

Two days later I called Marilyn for another appointment to talk over the final draft of her story. She said, "Come anytime, like, you know, for breakfast." There was in her voice a note which I had come to recognize—an appealing eagerness to please. I came again at ten and once again she slept till noon. Finally we sat down together on a tiny sofa. She was barefooted, wearing a robe, and had not yet washed off last night's mascara. Her delicate hair was in a sleep-tumbled whirl. But she had made me feel this was a compliment. "Friends," she had said, "accept you the way you are." As was usual, her face was very pale. She held the manuscript high in front of her eyes and carefully read it aloud, listening to every phrase to be sure it sounded exactly like her.

She kept the manuscript and I returned for it late that afternoon. On the steps of the house she showed me changes she had penciled in, all of them small. She asked me to take out a remark about quietly giving money to needy individuals.

And then we said goodbye. As I walked away she suddenly called after me, "Hey, thanks." I turned to look back and there she stood, very still and strangely forlorn. I thought then of her reaction earlier when I had asked if many friends had called up to rally round when she was fired by Fox. There was silence, and sitting very straight, eyes wide and hurt, she had answered with a tiny, "No."

MARILYN MONROE was an actress, model, global celebrity, and one of the twentieth century's most famous pop icons. Born in Los Angeles as Norma Jean Mortenson, she appeared in her first movie at age twenty-one and achieved breakout success in 1953. Monroe went on to appear in more than twenty films, including *Gentleman Prefer Blondes*, *The Seven Year Itch*, and *Some Like it Hot*.

SADY DOYLE is the author of *Trainwreck* and *Dead Blondes and Bad Mothers*. Her work has appeared in *In These Times*, *The Guardian*, *Elle. com*, *The Atlantic*, *Slate*, *Buzzfeed*, and *Rookie*, among other publications. She is the founder of the blog *Tiger Beatdown*, and won the first-ever Women's Media Center Social Media Award. She's been featured in *Rookie: Yearbook One and Yearbook Two*, and contributed to the *Book of Jezebel*. She lives in upstate New York.

ROBERT CAHN was a prominent American journalist and government advisor on environmental issues. Throughout a long career, he wrote and edited for *Collier's*, *Life*, the *Christian Science Monitor*, the *Saturday Evening Post*, *Reader's Digest*, the *Seattle Star*, and many more publications. Cahn won a Pulitzer Prize in 1969 for his work exploring the impact of tourism on national parks, and his work continues to influence environmental policy today.

HELEN HOVER WELLER was a prolific entertainment writer in Golden Age Hollywood. She covered gossip and wrote tabloid news about the biggest stars of the era, rubbing shoulders with the likes of Frank Sinatra, Humphrey Bogart, and Sammy Davis Jr. Her life is detailed in her daughter Sheila Weller's memoir *Dancing at Ciro's*, about the glamour and danger of the 1950s Sunset Strip.

WILLIAM THORNTON "PETE" MARTIN JR. was a longtime writer and editor for the *Saturday Evening Post*, where he became famous for his profiles of Hollywood celebrities. His "I Call On . . . " column featured interviews with Zsa Zsa Gabor, Lucille Ball, Grace Kelly, Bing Crosby, and others.

WILLIAM J. WEATHERBY was an acclaimed British journalist, novelist, and editor. He wrote for *The Guardian* and the *Sunday Times of London*, and served as an editor for Farrar, Straus & Giroux and Penguin Books. Among his many books are *James Baldwin: Artist on Fire* and *Conversations with Marilyn*.

RICHARD MERYMAN was a journalist and biographer who wrote and edited for *Life* magazine. He interviewed some of the greatest personalities of the twentieth century, including Charlie Chaplin, Elizabeth Taylor, Orson Welles, Louis Armstrong, Paul McCartney, Joan Rivers, and many, many others. Meryman wrote several biographies of his subjects, and his interview with Marilyn Monroe was adapted for television in 1992.

THE LAST INTERVIEW SERIES

KURT VONNEGUT:
THE LAST INTERVIEW

$15.95 / $17.95 CAN

978-1-61219-090-7
ebook: 978-1-61219-091-4

RAY BRADBURY:
THE LAST INTERVIEW

$15.95 / $15.95 CAN

978-1-61219-421-9
ebook: 978-1-61219-422-6

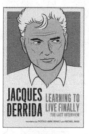

JACQUES DERRIDA:
THE LAST INTERVIEW:
LEARNING TO LIVE
FINALLY

$15.95 / $17.95 CAN

978-1-61219-094-5
ebook: 978-1-61219-032-7

JAMES BALDWIN:
THE LAST INTERVIEW

$15.95 / $15.95 CAN

978-1-61219-400-4
ebook: 978-1-61219-401-1

ROBERTO BOLAÑO:
THE LAST INTERVIEW

$15.95 / $17.95 CAN

978-1-61219-095-2
ebook: 978-1-61219-033-4

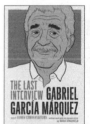

GABRIEL GÁRCIA
MÁRQUEZ: THE LAST
INTERVIEW

$15.95 / $15.95 CAN

978-1-61219-480-6
ebook: 978-1-61219-481-3

JORGE LUIS BORGES:
THE LAST INTERVIEW

$15.95 / $17.95 CAN

978-1-61219-204-8
ebook: 978-1-61219-205-5

LOU REED:
THE LAST INTERVIEW

$15.95 / $15.95 CAN

978-1-61219-478-3
ebook: 978-1-61219-479-0

HANNAH ARENDT:
THE LAST INTERVIEW

$15.95 / $16.95 CAN

978-1-61219-311-3
ebook: 978-1-61219-312-0

ERNEST HEMINGWAY:
THE LAST INTERVIEW

$15.95 / $20.95 CAN

978-1-61219-522-3
ebook: 978-1-61219-523-0

THE LAST INTERVIEW SERIES

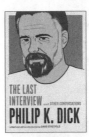

PHILIP K. DICK:
THE LAST INTERVIEW

$15.95 / $20.95 CAN

978-1-61219-526-1
ebook: 978-1-61219-527-8

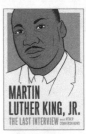

MARTIN LUTHER KING, JR.:
THE LAST INTERVIEW

$15.99 / $21.99 CAN

978-1-61219-616-9
ebook: 978-1-61219-617-6

NORA EPHRON:
THE LAST INTERVIEW

$15.95 / $20.95 CAN

978-1-61219-524-7
ebook: 978-1-61219-525-4

CHRISTOPHER HITCHENS:
THE LAST INTERVIEW

$15.99 / $20.99 CAN

978-1-61219-672-5
ebook: 978-1-61219-673-2

JANE JACOBS:
THE LAST INTERVIEW

$15.95 / $20.95 CAN

978-1-61219-534-6
ebook: 978-1-61219-535-3

HUNTER S. THOMPSON:
THE LAST INTERVIEW

$15.99 / $20.99 CAN

978-1-61219-693-0
ebook: 978-1-61219-694-7

DAVID BOWIE:
THE LAST INTERVIEW

$16.99 / $22.99 CAN

978-1-61219-575-9
ebook: 978-1-61219-576-6

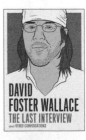

DAVID FOSTER WALLACE:
THE LAST INTERVIEW

$16.99 / 21.99 CAN

978-1-61219-741-8
ebook: 978-1-61219-742-5

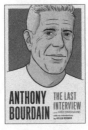

ANTHONY BOURDAIN:
THE LAST INTERVIEW

$16.99 / $22.99 CAN

978-1-61219-824-8
ebook: 978-1-61219-825-5

BILLIE HOLIDAY:
THE LAST INTERVIEW

$16.99 / 21.99 CAN

978-1-61219-741-8
ebook: 978-1-61219-742-5